W9-BAW-921

Sex & the New You

A Guide for the Christian Family

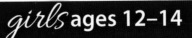

girls ages 12–14

For Discussion or Individual Use
Book 4 of the Learning about Sex Series for Girls

The titles in the series:

Book 1: Why Boys and Girls Are Different

Book 2: Where Do Babies Come From?

Book 3: How You Are Changing

Book 4: Sex and the New You

Book 5: Love, Sex, and God

Book 6: How to Talk Confidently with Your Child about Sex

Acknowledgments

We wish to thank all medical, child development, and family life consultants who have assisted in the development, updating, and revising of the Learning about Sex series.

Copyright © 1982, 1988, 1995, 1998, 2008, 2015
Concordia Publishing House
3558 S. Jefferson Ave., St. Louis, MO 63118-3968
1-800-325-3040 • www.cph.org

From text originally written by Richard Bimler

Unless otherwise noted, internal illustrations and photographs
© iStock.com.

Scripture quotations from the ESV Bible®
(The Holy Bible, English Standard Version®),
copyright © 2001 by Crossway Bibles,
a publishing ministry of Good News Publishers.
Used by permission. All rights reserved.

Manufactured in the United States of America/063692/412346

3 4 5 6 7 8 9 10 11   25 24 23 22 21 20 19 18 17

CONTENTS

Editors' Foreword

This book is one in a series of six designed to help parents communicate biblical values to their children in the area of sexuality. *Sex and the New You* is the fourth book in the series. It is written especially for girls ages 12 to 14 and, of course, for the parents, teachers, and other concerned adults who may want to discuss the book with the children in their care.

Like its predecessor, the updated Learning about Sex series provides information about the mental, emotional, physical, and spiritual aspects of human sexuality. Moreover, it does so from a distinctively Christian point of view, in the context of our relationship to the God who created us and redeemed us in Jesus Christ. The series presents sex as another good gift from God, and it helps us understand sex in the larger context of our entire life of faith. To counter cultural influences, be strong and consistent in communicating the miracle of God's design. The way God made us is just the way He knew it should be for our health and happiness.

Each book in the series is graded—in vocabulary and in the amount of information it provides. It answers the questions children at each age level typically ask. Because children vary widely in their growth rates and interest levels, parents and other concerned adults will want to preview each book in the series, directing each child to the next graded book when she is ready for it.

Ideally, this book will be used as part of a biblically based, broadly focused—yet personal—training that prepares young girls for womanhood. Young women grow and blossom into Christian womanhood through the teaching, training, and example provided by older women. A young woman can learn much from a mother, grandmother, or other adult woman who trusts in Jesus for her salvation. In the context of such a relationship, questions of a personal nature can be asked and answered, insightful discussions held, and godly behaviors modeled. Your expression of positive and God-pleasing values will likely have a greater impact on the healthy development of your daughter than any book, other than the Bible. God's plan unfolds as each generation in succession passes on the truths God imparts through His Word and the wisdom that comes as challenges are met and overcome by the power of God's grace through Christ. We pray that this will be the beginning of ongoing open, honest, and intentional communication with your child regarding God's magnificent design.

Note: The books in this series also can be used as mini units or as part of another course of study in a Christian school or church setting. Whenever the books are used in a class setting, it is important to let the parents know beforehand, since they have the primary responsibility for the sex education of their children. If used in a classroom setting, the books in this series are designed for separate single-gender groups, the setting most conducive to open conversations about questions and concerns. As the Christian home and the Christian school and church work together, Christian values in sex education can be more effectively strengthened.

You've Heard and You've Wondered

1

You've heard questions like those on page 6 before—maybe you've asked them yourself. And maybe you haven't been quite sure about the answers.

This book has been written to help you answer some of the questions you have about your body, about getting along with others, about sexuality, and about differences between males and females.

More important, this book will remind you who gave you life and made you who you are. You are a child of God. Because God loves you, He sent His own Son to live and die for you. This kind of love means He won't ever ignore you; He'll guide you and protect you and forgive you. Because Christ died for you and paid the penalty for your sins, God is able to accept you just as you are. And because Christ became a human being, He understands everything you are feeling and wondering about right now. He understands your questions about sex, your wonderings about your body, and your sexual daydreaming. He helps you to grow in a healthy relationship with Him, with other people, and with yourself.

He helps you to become a "new you."

Of course, reading this book won't automatically solve all your problems. You may still be disappointed with the way you look or the way you feel. But you will have the chance to look honestly at these things and to think and talk about them. You may wish you were different, but you will hear again and again that you were made by God—to be female, special, and unique!

On this page and the next are a few more of the questions people your age ask. Take a moment now to think of your own questions. If you want, write them down at the back of the book. Then, when you've finished the book, see whether they have been answered.

Questions I Wonder About

How do I know I am special to Jesus? See page 9.

How are babies born? See page 56.

Why don't I feel good about myself? See page 34.

©iStock.com / Steve Debenport

You're a Special Young Woman!

2

"Am I normal?" many young people ask. It's so easy to feel alone and different. It's easy to think you are the only person feeling the way you do—about your body, your family, yourself. Maybe you feel this way because of the changes in your body. Or you feel different because your body is not growing as fast as other girls around you. Or maybe your body grew much faster than the other girls, and that doesn't feel so good either. The last thing you want right now is to be different! Perhaps you are experiencing a growing awareness of sexual thoughts and feelings. You wonder if such thoughts are normal.

Who can I talk to?

It's good to have a friend you can talk with when you're not feeling good about yourself or are confused or sad. But it's especially great to know Jesus as our Friend! He can actually "sympathize with our weaknesses" because He "has been tempted as we are, yet without sin" (Hebrews 4:15). That's in the Bible, so we know it is true. Jesus really knows how we feel, because He was born and grew and went through the teen years too. That's why we can talk to Him and know He'll understand.

How do I know I am special to Jesus?

Even more, He's your Savior! He lived and died and rose again to make you a child of the heavenly Father. He's living proof that "the Father Himself loves you" (John 16:27). That's good to remember when you don't feel loved or when you feel guilty, anxious, or scared.

The God who loves you and forgives you is the same God who made you. No one else—not even an identical twin—is exactly like you. You are special; you are not a carbon copy of someone else. You look different, you feel different, you think differently than anyone else. You grow at a different rate—maybe in spurts, maybe at a fairly regular pace. But whatever your growth pattern, it's just right for you. Why? Because God made you and set your growing up into

In what ways has God made me different from anyone else in the world?

9

motion. When you recognize that God made you and loves you, it is okay to put your confidence in that fact. You are a child of God!

God gave you your body and soul, your eyes, ears, and all your members. He gave you your mind and senses, and He still takes care of them. How does He still take care of them? He gives your family resources to buy food, clothes, and a home where you can sleep. He gives you teachers who help you learn new things. He gives you the ability to think and choose healthy ways to take care of your body and mind. It is pretty neat to think that God's hand is in all these things.

Through these people and resources, you are able to be happy and healthy. And when you are happy and healthy, you, too, are able to serve other people as a daughter, a sister, and a friend. Taking care of your body and mind helps you serve!

How do I honor God in the care of my body?

Let's take a look at questions you can ask yourself that will help you to continue to be a healthy servant of God.

1. Do I get enough sleep every night? Would getting more sleep help me feel refreshed instead of tired?

2. Do I eat nourishing food? Is the food I eat helping my body grow? Do I sometimes eat too little or too much?

3. Do I wash my body and face every day to keep myself clean and free from germs?

4. Do I care for my body by exercising in healthy ways—not too much and not too little?

5. Do I recognize that smoking is not something that will keep my body healthy?

6. Do I believe that taking drugs and drinking alcohol can cause me to make poor decisions?

To which of the following do you relate?

☐ "What is happening to my body?"

☐ "Why isn't my body changing yet?"

☐ "I feel like I am too tall."

☐ "I feel like I am too short."

☐ "I'm so awkward! I keep tripping over my feet!"

☐ "My voice cracks."

☐ "My face has zits."

☐ "No one else has the problems I have; no one ever did."

☐ "No one understands me."

☐ "I don't understand me."

Food, exercise, staying clean, sleeping, not smoking or taking drugs, not drinking alcohol, continuing to learn all that you can in school: all these things contribute to keeping the body God gave you healthy. He doesn't care if you have pimples or are the prettiest girl in the world. He cares for you through all these things and equips you to help your mom, to have fun with your friends, to help a neighbor with her lawn, or to tutor your younger brother in reading. Things like this are how we serve one another. Being healthy helps you do this!

By taking care of your body, you also show glory to God, who created you. Paul wrote a letter to other Christians and encouraged them: "Do you not know that your body is a temple of the Holy Spirit within you, whom you have from God? You are not your own, for you were bought with a price. So glorify God in your body" (1 Corinthians 6:19–20).

Even if you have pimples right now, even if you feel clumsy and awkward, even if you don't like how you look on the outside, remember that you belong to God and that He loves you. Peek in the mirror again. Go ahead—it won't hurt. Look beyond the familiar surface and find the hand of God there. See if you don't feel a little different now—ready to go and serve others because that is WHY God made you.

You are chosen by God. You've been set apart from other people in this world. You are God's child, a member of His family, working together to bring God glory.

> What difference does being a Christian make?

You are different than others. Our culture puts out confusing messages about your identity, your body, and your sexuality. But in His Word, God tells us His will—what is best for us. He knows, because He made us! In His Word, He tells us that He would do anything for us because He loves us.

The world may tell you to live for the moment because you only live once. The world may tell you that you have the right to choose to do whatever you want with your body. But the world is full of the consequences of those selfish, sinful attitudes: addiction, death, unplanned pregnancies, broken relationships, and emotional pain.

The Holy Spirit is helping you to make good choices to keep your growing mind and your growing faith healthy. He will strengthen you. The Holy Spirit is also helping you to make good choices to keep your growing body healthy.

You may feel like you're the only one who isn't watching "those" shows or listening to "that kind" of music. Or you may worry that your friends will make fun of you. But chances are that you aren't the only one of your friends who feels uncomfortable when someone in your group shows something inappropriate. Try to stay busy with activities that you know are not questionable. Suggest to your friends doing a different activity instead of watching an improper show or movie.

If you are a Christian, God's Spirit lives in your body. You are a valuable member of God's family. It matters what you put into your body. Remember, "You are not your own, for you were bought with a price. So glorify God in your body" (1 Corinthians 6:19–20).

Excessive use of alcohol and drugs does permanent damage to brain cells. Any use of alcohol and drugs interferes with your thinking and can cause you to make really bad choices that you might regret for a long time afterward.

Does it matter? Isn't it my body and my choice?

Smoking can lead to serious problems, such as lung or oral cancer and heart disease. Smokers have bad breath, their clothes smell, and their teeth can become yellow. Other tobacco products such as chewing tobacco are not safer. They, too, can cause gum disease and cancer. Smokeless tobacco irritates your gum tissue and can cause tooth decay, and it is even more addictive than cigarettes.

Other people are affected by the choices you make about your body. If you smoke, the people who live in your home and who are around you will suffer the physical effects of breathing in the smoke that comes from the end of your cigarettes. This secondhand smoke can cause ear infections, lung or breathing problems, asthma attacks, or even cancer. A mother who smokes, drinks alcohol, or does drugs is much more likely than those who don't to bear children who have serious physical and mental problems.

Those who abuse alcohol or drugs often cause accidents that harm others. As a preoccupation with alcohol and drugs takes control of them, they waste their lives, are unproductive, and destroy their relationships. Support of an illegal drug culture leads to many other terrible crimes.

As the Holy Spirit works through God's Word, He gives us the power to honor God in the choices we make about what we put into our bodies and how we care for them. He helps us to live our life for Jesus—the one who lived, died, and now lives again for us! As Christians, we can look to the future instead of living for the moment. You can think through what will happen if you make a certain choice. And you can have peace knowing that no matter how much of a struggle it is to live as a Christian in this world, you don't live only once. This world is not the best that it gets. Our human minds can't even imagine the joys that await us in heaven, and through the Holy Spirit at work in us, that's where our focus lies.

Critical Thinking:

- The stage you are in right now is called *adolescence*. Does it feel like an awkward time? Why is God having you go through these changes?

- Look back at your day or week. What are some ways you have made poor choices that show you were only thinking about yourself? What are some ways you thought about others and served them (like a parent, brother, sister, friend, or teacher)? How can you change the way you do things so you focus more on showing God's love by serving others?

- If you feel bad about the way you have behaved and the choices you made, what do you think happens next for a Christian? (Hint: Tell God you are sorry and know that you are forgiven!)

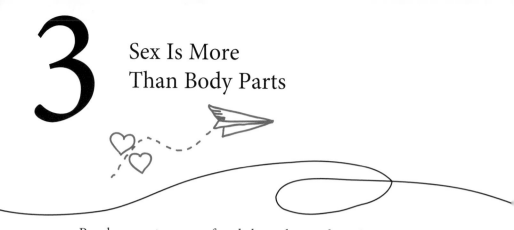

3 Sex Is More Than Body Parts

People can get very confused about the word *sex*. It can mean either "gender" or "intercourse." Many people use *sex* to refer to the act of intercourse or to physical attraction between men and women. Basically, sex—whether a person is male or female—is determined by the type of reproductive body parts an individual has, but it is also determined by the very makeup of our cells. Our brains are wired differently, so males and females don't look at and process things the same way. We are not just male and female in sexual organs but in and throughout our entire body, mind, and spirit. God made you female from the moment of conception.

Our culture tends to use many terms loosely and interchangeably, but sometimes this creates confusion. For example, some people use the terms *sex* and *gender* as if they have the same meaning. But the term *sex* is a way to designate the biological fact that we are male or female. *Gender* often describes how a person feels about her sex; it relates to one's self-perception. Anywhere you go, biological sex differences remain the same, but gender roles, behaviors, and attributes may differ, depending on the culture. What a culture (or a larger group) believes is appropriate for males and females can differ from group to group or society to society.

What is gender?

What makes this especially confusing is that some people in our culture today don't like the basic male and female distinctions in sex and are working to create many new genders. Some say there are seven genders and others as many as fifty-six! But, if gender describes how people perceive themselves, they can also be confused about this. If a woman believes herself to be a man, we might think she has "gender identity disorder," which is a psychological condition.

Another term to describe this condition is **transgender**, which means that a person does not identify with his or her biological sex. Society today is moving away from seeing a transgender condition as a disorder and more to celebrating a person no matter how she thinks of herself. There are several different ways people express themselves as transgender:

A **transsexual** person tries to look, dress, and act like a member of the opposite sex. The person may have been born male, for instance, but identifies with being female. The person may even have surgery to remove biological sex organs and have organs of the opposite sex created instead.

Transvestites, or people who cross-dress, are usually comfortable with the sex God created them to be, but they like to wear clothing that is typically worn by the opposite sex.

Not all people who seem genderless—neither having specifically masculine or feminine characteristics (also called **androgynous**)— or who seem gender nonconforming are transgender persons.

Homosexuality means sexual attraction to those of the same sex. Homosexuals include men who are attracted to men and women who are attracted to women. Often, a homosexual person is said to be gay. Women homosexuals also are called lesbians. Heterosexuals are sexually attracted to the opposite sex—a man who is sexually attracted to a woman or a woman who is sexually attracted to a man.

What does it mean to be gay?

To be attracted to a person of the opposite sex is part of God's design to bring male and female together. The world around you is often telling you a message that is not a part of God's design. This message says, "If you are attracted to someone, it is okay to have sex with that person." This is not true.

15

God's design places the act of sex within marriage. He does this because it is His good will to do so, to provide a spouse who will vow to love and support you for the rest of your life and to provide the possibility that you will have children. Within this lifelong marriage, you will love and care for your children. This is God's design.

However, we can understand that some people feel a sexual attraction for members of their same sex. To say someone has same-sex attractions is a helpful way to understand what is happening in her life. If those attractions are strong and persistent, some people will then say they have a homosexual orientation. However, having an attraction does not mean that people *must* act sexually on that attraction, any more than a married woman *must* act on her attraction to a man other than her husband (which can happen). It also does not mean that your sexual interest in a boy means that you must be sexually active with him. When people say they did not choose to be gay, this is partly correct. They most certainly did not choose whether they would be sexually attracted to their same sex or the opposite sex. However, everyone has a choice on whether to *act* on those attractions and whether to adopt a gay identity. Our culture tells people, especially young people, that if they have same-sex attractions they not only must *act* on them, but they must *be* gay. Unfortunately, this can be harmful to many people. Research shows that as many as 25 percent of young people are confused about or question their sexuality at some point while growing up. As adults, however, only 2–3 percent of people identify as gay or lesbian. *That is a big difference.*

You are going through tremendous changes right now, with massive hormonal influences that are often difficult to understand and manage. Confusion at some point in this process is normal, but it doesn't need to lead you to make choices that go against your faith or the biological reality that you are created by God to be female.

Why are some people gay?

Researchers continue to disagree on the specific "causes" of homosexuality, but they mostly agree that there is a complex interaction between genetics and environmental factors in childhood. However it happens seems to be unique for each person, but there can be some points of commonality among people who feel same-sex attractions, including feeling a distance from the parent of the same sex or early childhood sexual abuse.

The majority of gay men and lesbians say they felt little or no choice about their sexual attraction.

No one can know for certain why this is. Christians view homosexuality by what God's Word tells us. In the Bible, we see that God created people as male and female. We do not see terms like *heterosexual* and *homosexual*, even if the Bible does talk about sinful sexual behavior. In that sense, God's Word is clear that homosexual behavior is not what God wants for His children. When He created Adam and Eve, He made them different—male and female—so they fit together. This is part of God's design for our sexual organs. They fit together too. God also gave man and woman to each other to be married, so they could support and help each other, and to form a family where children are created and brought into the world. Homosexual relationships that include children automatically deny those children a mother or a father, something that clearly violates God's design. The real bottom line: whenever people have sex outside of a marriage between one man and one woman, they go against God's will. Most people experience sexual attraction prior to getting married, including those with same-sex attractions. However, because of their faith in Jesus Christ, Christians do not act on these attractions. Those who never get married or those who have same-sex attractions may struggle with this temptation for their entire lives, but they have chosen to honor God, despite their difficulties.

How should I treat a person who is gay?

Remember, too, that no one can identify who has same-sex attractions by outward appearances. Often, people are called homosexual for reasons based on hatred, suspicion, or just being mean. It is not uncommon for teens to feel confusion about sexual identity. Kids your age hear and see a lot of messages in our culture that say that having sex with anyone you like is perfectly okay. You are likely dealing with a lot of strong hormones and changes in your body. It is sometimes hard to sort out all your feelings. You love the girlfriend you have been playing with since preschool. Does that mean you're gay?

Having these thoughts does not mean you are a lesbian. Nor does finding pleasure in activities that aren't typical for girls mean that you are not feminine or attracted to boys. There are many athletic and physically strong girls. The important thing to remember is that if you are having struggles, you can talk with your parents, your pastor, or another trusted, mature Christian adult. In addition to listening, the adult will likely share with you that God made you female and very good, that you are growing into a young woman, and that God loves you.

The most important thing to know is this—Christ died and rose again to forgive all sinners. This includes everybody, those who deal with same-sex attraction and those who are attracted to the opposite sex. We should treat people who struggle with same-sex attraction as we would any other person. They, too, are redeemed by Christ. If someone with a same-sex attraction chooses to have a sexual relationship, they are choosing to disobey God. And if someone attracted to the opposite sex chooses to have a sexual relationship outside of marriage, they, too, are disobeying God. As Christians, we don't approve of any sinful choices, but we still show love to all because we are sinners too.

In His Word, God says clearly what things are wrong, and He says clearly that sin is forgiven in Christ. Both homosexuals and heterosexuals can be guilty of sinful lusts. But God calls all people to repentance—to admit and be sorry about sin, to receive the forgiveness Jesus offers, and to turn away from sin and lead a godly life through the power of the Holy Spirit at work in us. No one who asks for forgiveness is beyond receiving it fully. Only the love of God in Jesus and the power He brings can give you the strength to reject temptation and to reach out in forgiveness and Christian love.

As a friend, you can encourage others to read God's Word to better understand sin and its power. Share with all your friends the Good News that because Christ loves them, He died for them and for you. You do not need to judge or be mean, but serve and invite them to return to God's Word for help and understanding. God's Word is "the power of God for salvation" (Romans 1:16) for all sinners.

> What are some parts of your body you thank God for?

It is wonderful to have both male and female. We are all human, but we are also unique and distinct according to our sex. That's the way God wanted it to be. These differences do not mean that one sex is better than the other. It just means that God made male and female with sex-related characteristics and organs. We can celebrate and thank God for this good design. For Christians, however, our sexuality involves more than just body parts and design. It's how we feel about and use our body parts as good gifts of God. All parts of our bodies are good and useful. In fact, we understand that certain parts of our bodies have a higher honor, and we take special care of them (1 Corinthians 12:23).

Even a child who knows the proper names for those parts needs to learn when and where to use the names. Many people use nicknames for *penis* or *vagina* in vulgar stories or jokes. But that doesn't mean these parts are dirty. How could anything God made be dirty? It's the misuse and abuse of these body parts that is wrong. Thanking God for your body includes thanking Him for everything that makes you who you are—your vagina as well as your eyes and ears.

When God first created people, He made them perfect. That means their bodies were perfect—every part of their bodies. God Himself said all His creation was "good." But when He created the first people, He said this was "very good." (See Genesis 1:31.) Take a moment now to look at your hand. Open and close your fingers slowly. Note the precision with which they move—instantly, simply on the command of your mind. What machine can be so gentle and yet as strong as a human hand? Picture the marvelous things that hands can do: dribble a basketball or move over a keyboard. Think of a surgeon's hands skillfully manipulating instruments in open-heart surgery or a mother's hands gently stroking her baby's face.

Think of your eye—more wonderful than a camera. It sees color and motion, adjusts itself to dim light or bright sun, focuses automatically, never needs film, and develops its pictures instantly. As we'll see in the next chapter, your sex organs are just as wonderfully made as your hand or your eye. For God Himself "arranged the members in the body, each one of them, as He chose" (1 Corinthians 12:18).

Still, we regard our sex organs differently than we regard body parts such as hands or eyes. Paul refers to sex organs as "unpresentable" parts that "are treated with greater modesty" (1 Corinthians 12:23). The way you dress and your attitudes toward privacy and sexuality are a part of what Paul calls "greater modesty." God designed our bodies in just the right way to make us fit to help and serve others. You are magnificently designed by a loving Creator. Right now, you will use your mind, your emotions, your hands, and your words to care for others. Someday, you may use your sexual organs to care for a husband and perhaps even to have children.

How do you treat your "unpresentable" parts differently?

All your body parts work together to help you serve at the appropriate times and to the people God gives you to serve. You can feel good about the many things your body can and will do! You can feel good about being a female.

Your sex—your female body design—is an important gift from God. He made you that way for His own purpose—to love and serve others. Because you are a female, you have many unique gifts from God. You may be a mother someday. You may be very nurturing and expressive with your emotions. You may be weaker and gentler than a man. Does that mean that you are less than a man? No, you are just made differently. As your body changes, so do the hormones that contribute to your emotions. Some days you feel great; other days you feel sad or angry. Your hormones are changing now, so you should not be surprised that your emotions are changing too. This can be difficult at times, but it is a normal part of growing up.

As a boy's hormone levels start to change, they might be tempted to do more reckless or aggressive things. As their strength increases, they might be tempted to use their power in hurtful ways. You, too, can remember to be aware of your emotions and what triggers strong feelings. It's important to be in control of our emotions and not let them control our bodies. How do you control your emotions? Prayer and quiet devotional time with God and personal Bible study are great ways. God's Word will strengthen and encourage you during this time of questioning, learning, and growing. He will help you keep things under control!

More important than the physical changes is the growth you will experience in responsibility, integrity, maturity in decision-making, and wisdom as God's Spirit guides you. Talk with your parents about these key characteristics. Your mom or another Christian woman can help guide you toward the responsibility, integrity, maturity, and wisdom of a young Christian woman. With God's blessing and through His Word, you will also continue to grow in faith as His own dear child.

You are a gift of God; He made you as you are so you can be a blessing to others and to Him. It's a challenge and a joy to be a Christian woman. From the very beginning, God designed women to care for and nurture things in His creation. Women take care of others; it is a part of our design. You will feel joy as you use your God-given gifts to serve others. What are the things you do that serve or give care to your parents? your siblings? your teachers? your friends? Sometimes no one notices the things you do. That's okay! It is a part of a servant attitude that God desires. You serve not because someone will notice but because someone needs you.

What does a servant look like? The greatest servant was Jesus Christ. He lived in perfect obedience to God's will, died to earn our forgiveness and salvation, and rose again in victory over sin and death. His unselfish sacrifice gives us the blessing of forgiveness now and life with Him eternally when we die. What a relief that our salvation and resurrection are already taken care of! It is why we can take care of others here on earth.

Critical Thinking:

- If you often go out in public wearing tight or revealing clothes, what message are you sending to males?

- If you make fun of people who are different than you (e.g., people with same-sex attractions, girls who have masculine characteristics, boys who are smaller than you), what are you saying to Jesus about the people He has died for? What message are you sending about God's creation (that person)?

- If Jesus died for all sinners and loves all of us, how does this change you? How can you feel about the opportunity to serve others? Who are the people who serve you? Whom do you serve? How do you serve them?

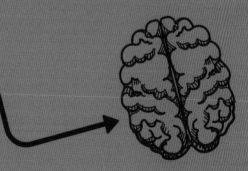

4 Men and Women Are Different, Aren't They?

Sure, men and women are different. Recent studies by psychologists show that there are differences even between very young boy babies and girl babies. For example, girl babies respond sooner than boy babies to the voices and faces of their parents. Boy babies are more likely to be able to scan the whole room and notice nearby objects. On average, adult men see better than women in daytime, but women see better at night. But these and many other differences are average differences. They won't predict whether a certain man or woman can see better in daytime. Nor are the inborn differences between the genders very great.

God created men and women to be different, but the differences were designed to bring them together, not to separate them. Because men and women were created to *complement* (to add to in order to improve) one another, they relate with others, communicate, and love differently. Generally, females are more comfortable talking and sharing how they feel than men (we call that being more verbal). Girls build relationships as they connect with others using feelings. Boys and men are more likely to communicate and build relationships around actions and activities (that would be nonverbal). Women are verbal; men are nonverbal. When you put the two together, there is an addition of something different that works to improve the situation—that's complementing!

> In what ways are men and women the same?

The most obvious differences between men and women are physical. But the physical differences were not meant to set a limit on things that are not physical. A woman might not be able to lift or carry as much weight as most men, but that doesn't mean she can't drive a moving van or manage a moving company as well as or better than many men. A man might not have spent as much time in a kitchen as a woman while growing up, but that doesn't mean he can't wash the dishes, do the laundry, or plan and prepare a seven-course dinner.

Remember, we are talking here about characteristics of women and men on average, not a specific woman or man. This is important because you may be a nonverbal girl. There isn't anything wrong with you. You are no less of a female. You may have other characteristics that aren't typical for a girl. That doesn't make you a boy, does it?

As girls grow into women and as boys grow into men, they are often expected to have the characteristics usually associated with their sex. The trouble is, when we say all women and all men are or have to be a certain way, we may keep some individuals from using the good gifts and talents God has given them. For example:

- **Eva is a fourteen-year-old super athlete having trouble getting on a baseball team. Baseball teams are for boys, right?**
- **Javier enjoys cooking, but his brother says it's a "girl's job." Cooking is for girls, right?**
- **Elena loves to work on her dad's car. Some neighbors don't think that hobby is very "ladylike." Being a mechanic is man's work, right?**

With God's design for females in mind, we still celebrate that each of us is unique. No one is just like you. You can usually tell by looking whether a person is a boy or a girl, but each one of us is still different, and that is a beautiful thing!

God has given all people gifts of all kinds to use in His service and in the service of others. What gifts has God given you? How will you use them in a way that is respectful of God's plan for womanhood?

In a letter to Timothy, the apostle Paul describes God's will regarding the behavior of young women and men. God's plan is for women to dress "in respectable apparel, with modesty and self-control, not with braided hair and gold or pearls or costly attire, but with what is proper for women who profess godliness—with good works" (1 Timothy 2:9–10).

What is God's will for young women?

Men "should pray, lifting holy hands without anger or quarreling" (1 Timothy 2:8) and "pursue righteousness, godliness, faith, love, steadfastness, and gentleness. Fight the good fight of the faith. Take hold of the eternal life to which you were called and about which you made the good confession in the presence of many witnesses" (1 Timothy 6:11–12).

When we teach and interact with others, God's Word commands us, "Let no one despise you for your youth, but set the believers an example in speech, in conduct, in love, in faith, in purity" (1 Timothy 4:12).

As you grow to be a Christian woman, you will have many ways to serve others. God gives you opportunities to serve now and is working in your life to prepare you for future service. He will continue to train you in godliness (1 Timothy 4:7) as you continue to learn about Jesus from the Bible and from worshiping with your family in church.

You will grow in modesty and self-control as you choose to honor God with your body and mind. You will be tempted to do things that are not godly. The Holy Spirit will give you self-control to resist. You can choose clothing that keeps your private body parts private and behaviors that maintain sexual purity. This modesty protects you and maintains the highest respect for yourself and others. One way you can serve the young men in your life is to recognize how they are drawn visually to women's bodies and appearance. God did design attraction to work this way, but young men can abuse that God-given attraction. You are not responsible for the sexual purity of their thoughts or actions, of course. Men need to pray for and work diligently at practicing self-control to bring their desires in line with Christ. But you are responsible for your own choices and actions, fully aware of how your choices impact others for good or ill. You can pray for and work diligently at practicing similar self-control. The apostle Paul warned the Corinthians to "take care that this right of yours does not somehow become a stumbling block to the weak" (1 Corinthians 8:9). Just because you're able to do something does not make it right, because your actions affect others.

> As God's children through faith in Christ Jesus, we are called to respect and appreciate the difference between men and women. At the same time, we are to respect and appreciate the similarities and never demonstrate demeaning, diminishing, or degrading attitudes toward one another.

Honestly examine your interests and your abilities in light of God's will for you as His child. Are you quiet and shy? Perhaps you can help out in the church nursery. Are you athletic and boisterous? Perhaps you can help coach a girls' soccer team. Do you like books? Perhaps you can practice writing now to be a Christian writer of books like this one. Ask God's Spirit for the power and ability to examine your life and make choices that reflect that you are a child of God, equipped for service by the love and forgiveness of Jesus, who died for you and rose again. Whatever you do now as a girl, and whatever you choose to do as you grow into a young woman, "work heartily, as for the Lord" (Colossians 3:23).

Critical Thinking:

- In what ways are men and women different?

- What unique gifts or talents has God given you? (Ask your mom or dad if you get stuck; they'll know what they are!)

- How might you use your unique gifts to serve other people now? when you are an adult?

5 Is Sex a Secret?

Have you ever noticed that most people don't usually like to talk about sex? Have you kind of tried to bring it up with a mom, grandmother, or aunt? A lot of people never talk about sex. It makes people uncomfortable. Funny, isn't it? Because you know that sex is everywhere you look: TV, movies, the mall, Internet, social media, music, at school.

You might be able to make the situation a little easier by asking your mom (or an aunt or a woman you trust) questions you have to get the conversation started. It might be difficult. Your mom might be thinking it just isn't the right time yet. But you know you have questions, and you may be a bit confused about the answers your friends or the Internet are giving you.

How do I talk about sex? It's tough.

Try making a list of questions that you'd like to ask, and find a time to ask when nothing else is interfering. Don't ask all of your questions at once; try one, and see if that breaks the ice. This is a chance to show your parents you are growing up and want to talk to them in a mature way. It's a good way to improve family communications and to help your family grow together.

Parents aren't the only ones you can get information from. You probably know another adult—a pastor, counselor, teacher, or relative—whom you like and who might be willing to listen to your questions. Sometimes friends can be helpful, but often they don't know any more about sex than you do. Even those friends who seem to talk most freely about sex may be giving you more imagination than facts. And you want facts.

Obviously, there's a lot of talk about sex in school, but so much of it gives sex a bad name. Some people use slang terms, dirty jokes, and degrading laughter to cover their own embarrassment, lack of information, and misconceptions about sex. There's a lot of talk about sex in music and in the media, but again, it just adds to the misconceptions. Such activity cheapens God's wonderful gift and increases the misunderstandings many young people have.

> **Who are people you could talk to about sex?**

> **Does talking about it cheapen God's gift of sex?**

I could talk to my dad.

Young people sometimes do things connected with sex or think about sex in a way that they know is wrong. They feel guilty and know that they have done something wrong. As a result, they can feel very sorry for what they've thought or done. Feeling guilty about sex comes from an awareness of failure to obey God's Law. Your parents have been teaching you what God says is right and wrong. This is part of how they take care of you. But without them ever really having to say it, you know that you are too young to be involved in sexual acts or to view images that are sexual in nature. As you grow up to be a woman, you will be tempted and may sometimes do things that are wrong that you have never done before. Some of these may be related to sex, such as looking at pictures that you know you shouldn't or going on the Internet to find images about sex because you are curious or your friends told you about them. Doing these things will probably make you feel bad too.

What if I feel really guilty?

These feelings serve a purpose, just like guilty feelings about other things you do wrong. You say something nasty to your parents, you cheat on a test, you lie about something else, and you feel guilty. Sexual sins are no different from other sins in the eyes of God. They are all wrong.

But the great thing about being a Christian is that God the Judge is also God the Forgiver. God the Father sent His Son to die for all your sins. With His resurrection came the victory over the power of sin. Feeling guilty makes you look for help. Thank God that Jesus brings help and forgiveness. Trust His Word to you: "Your sins are forgiven. . . . Go in peace" (Luke 7:48, 50).

Jesus also said, "Sin no more" (John 8:11), but you know you're going to sin again. We all do! That doesn't mean it is okay to sin or to sin more. In fact, when God forgives you, He also gives you the power to live a new life. This is the special work of the Holy Spirit. Through God's Word, the Holy Spirit strengthens you against the temptation to sin. You can read the Bible, go to church, and start preparing for Holy Communion at church. The Holy Spirit also gives the power to confess (to apologize) to God and to others when you do something wrong.

And, above all, He gives the assurance that forgiveness is already yours because Christ died for you and paid the price for all your sins. Knowing this makes you totally free to live a new life because of Christ—to thankfully serve Him by serving others and by avoiding sin.

Sex is also given a bad name because some people distort God's gift of sex for their own pleasure so much that they physically and emotionally hurt another person. **Sexual abuse** happens when a person asserts power and authority over another—usually a child—to obtain sexual pleasure. The abuser might be an older child or an adult. In a sexual abuse situation, the abuser might kiss the child in a sexual way, touch the child on the **genitals**, make the child touch him or her, or even have sexual intercourse with the child. Sexual abuse is always the fault of the abuser and never the fault of the child or the abused.

Most children will not be abused, but all children need to be careful. If someone says or does something that makes you feel uncomfortable, it's important to tell your parents or another adult you trust right away. Don't keep anything bottled up inside you!

In most cases, the child who was abused knows the person who abused him or her. However, there are important things for you to know and rules to follow:

> - **Be aware that sometimes abusers use the Internet to get to know their victims.**
> - **Never give your name, address, or other information about yourself to someone over the Internet.**
> - **Never meet in person with anyone you've met online but have never seen in person before.**

Those who take sexual advantage of others are committing a crime. If you know this is happening, you should tell your parents right away. They will take care of reporting the person who is doing this so that he or she can be stopped and get the help he or she needs.

Remember that God created you to be His child. There is nothing that could happen that would change His love for you. Because of this, you can love and respect yourself, too, and insist that others treat you with respect.

Sex (the act of intercourse) and your sexuality (or female gender) is a precious gift from God. It should be treated with great respect and discussed in ways that bring glory to God. After all, our bodies are temples of the Holy Spirit

What do I need to know about sexual abuse?

What does it mean that my body is the temple of the Holy Spirit?

29

(1 Corinthians 6:19). The Holy Spirit dwells inside you. In the Old Testament, God dwelled within the tabernacle or the temple in order to be with His people. In fact, it was in a very special place inside these structures called the Most Holy Place. Only the chief priest was allowed to enter this special place and only once a year. In this holy place, the priest offered a sacrifice at the mercy seat of God to atone for the sins of all the people for that entire year.

This special place, this special function of the priest, and this special sacrifice all pointed to Christ, His special work, and His special sacrifice on the cross. Jesus was both the priest and the sacrifice that atoned for all sins of all people for all time! When Jesus said, "It is finished!" on the cross, He meant that there was no more need for the temple, the chief priest, or the yearly sacrifices. He did it all!

But when Jesus left this earth, ascending to heaven, He gave a gift to His people to remind them of all He taught and accomplished for them. This special gift is called "the Comforter," God the Holy Spirit. God no longer dwells in a special physical place where only one man can visit once a year. The Holy Spirit—God—dwells inside you. You are that special place, a holy place.

What a special gift to know that the Holy Spirit dwells in us, and what a special privilege we have to honor His holy presence within us. The Holy Spirit comes to you through the Word of God. We know that this Word of God is the power that makes Baptism a very special gift from God. In Baptism, the Word and the water combine. In Baptism, we receive the Holy Spirit, forgiveness of sins, and eternal life.

Even with the Holy Spirit dwelling in us, we do still sin, and that sin produces guilt. It might be helpful to think of the guilt you feel when you sin as a gift of God. How can this be? Because feeling ashamed of sin is evidence of the work of the Holy Spirit within you. God does not desire that you remain in your guilt, but that you quickly repent of your sin, confess it, and receive His forgiveness. In this way, the Spirit of God helps you every day to stay in a right relationship with God. This is the abundant grace of God given to us by the Holy Spirit dwelling within us—He is always with us, always helping us, always forgiving us, and always praying for us within His new temple (our bodies)!

When you have questions about any aspect of your body, be sure to seek answers from those who share your faith in Jesus. Like you, they will believe in the forgiveness Christ earned and the presence of the Holy Spirit with us. Talk to a trusted adult who knows the answers to your questions, is willing to talk, treats sexual terminology and attitudes with respect, and thanks God for making you who and what you are.

Critical Thinking:

- Why do you think people don't like to talk about sex? Whom can you talk to about sex?

- Why should you tell a trusted adult if someone touches you in a sexual way?

- How can you honor the Holy Spirit right now with choices and behaviors that treat His gift of sex as special? Who gives you the power to do these things?

6 You're Changing into a New You

You probably don't need the title of this chapter to know that its words are true. You probably knew something was different when your clothes didn't fit anymore. Or when you had trouble not tripping as you walked across a level floor. Or maybe when your moments of depression or frustration increased. No, you probably don't need a book to tell you that you're changing. You see it, feel it, and sense it all the time.

How do I stop worrying about things?

It's called **adolescence**, and it is the time of changing from a child into an adult. It is a very necessary trip; puberty is the name of this first stage in adolescence, when a person first becomes physically capable of reproducing. Often, the trip to adulthood will be exciting for you, but it also will be frustrating both to you and to others, mostly because of the changes happening in you and your concerns about them. Since joy and frustration are both part of adolescence, think of this time as an opportunity to draw closer to God and those who love you. They can help guide you through these difficult times.

Your body is changing, and so is your personality. You feel more strongly about big things and little things. You want to be more involved in decisions. You want to be on your own to try out some new ideas, to do some new things. It's all part of growing up. At times, you'll feel pulled in both directions. Half the time, you'll want the freedom of an adult, and half the time, you'll want the security of a child.

Recognizing your feelings is important during this time in your life. Perhaps you will find comfort in journaling your thoughts each night. Prayer will be a special time for you as you process your feelings; Jesus brings "peace that surpasses all understanding"—more calm and contentment than you can imagine (Philippians 4:7). Your loving heavenly Father knows your cares and burdens, and He knows your needs and provides for you. "Even the hairs of your head are all numbered" (Matthew 10:30).

The best thing you can do is remember who you are. God made you, and He cares and provides for you at each stage of your growing from baby to girl to woman. Jesus, your Savior, promises always to love and forgive you and to guide and remain with you along life's path. Use adolescence as a time to discover who you are and to develop your own style, appreciate your personality, and respect the body you've been given. Be who you are—in Him!

Who am I? Who do I want to be?

As you work at finding out what and who you are, you're going to look around at others. You'll see some people who are what you want to be and many who aren't. Use these models to shape your actions, but don't lose yourself in the process. Heroes and role models are fine, but remember that you are you, and most of what you're going to be will come from inside you, not from anyone else.

It's so easy to assume that popularity depends on who you are, what you have, or how you look. But you'll find more often that it's based on how you treat, respect, and act toward others. Be yourself, without ever forgetting that others are important too. God has given you a lot. Your happiness will depend on how well you use those gifts and how comfortable you are with them. You will feel most content with life when you're happy with what God has given you, both your body and your experiences. It feels great to make the most of what you have. The Holy Spirit helps you trust that God knows what's best for you and helps you to be thankful for all His blessings. The best thing for you to "wear" is a positive attitude!

Your Body Is Changing

When will I change?

Most of us have a time in life when we grow very rapidly. This is called a growth spurt. You already may have begun a growth spurt. You may still be waiting. You don't need to worry if it hasn't hit you yet—it will. You'll almost be able to see your legs get longer. You'll outgrow your clothes before you wear them out.

Most girls enter this stage between ages 9 and 12; boys usually enter it later, most often between ages 11 and 14. It's not at all unusual for girls to be taller than boys during the junior high years. It might be a little embarrassing or awkward that this happens just when boys and girls start noticing each other, but usually by age 15, boys catch up and grow taller than most girls.

You'll become much more aware of your height and weight during these years. Some youth will measure, weigh, and compare with others frequently, but you don't have to be concerned and do this. You don't need to worry when you don't seem to be growing as fast as others or when others aren't growing as fast as you are. Differences in growth rate are common—and normal. God is in control of your develop-ment, and you can trust that He knows what's best for you and for each person. He made you and He knows everything!

Why don't I feel good about myself?

Few girls are exactly the size they'd like to be. Some are larger than their mothers, but not all. You may be the tallest in your class or the shortest. You may be heavier or lighter than you would like. Most girls will gain five to six pounds per year around age 15, and after that maybe six or eight pounds per year. Boys will add twelve to twenty pounds per year by age 14 or 15, and after that maybe six or eight pounds per year. Heredity has a lot to do with this, but so does what and how you eat. Your hands and feet will grow first, then your arms and legs, and then the rest of your body.

Sometimes, your body will grow so fast that your tendons and ligaments become tighter. Tendons connect muscle to bone and ligaments connect bone to bone or cartilage to bone. Some people call this tightness and achiness *growing pains*. One way to decrease the pain is to be sure to stretch before and after exercise.

The main thing to remember is that differences in height and weight and rate of development are normal—and good. Imagine a world where all of us matured at exactly the same rate and wound up exactly the same size and shape. What a bore! God knew what He was doing when He made each person unique. Where would basketball be if everyone could dunk the ball or if no one could? Where would that sport be without the quick little guards darting between the big guys? And where would it be without all those who participate in the game as spectators?

There's a place for everyone and a role for everyone. You might excel as an athlete, musician, writer, computer whiz, artist, or something else. Try them all until you find the one that fits best; then accept it, and do the best you can in that role. You can use the gifts God has given you to serve others in ways that brings you joy, instead of wishing you had different gifts.

How will I change?

One of the changes during puberty and adolescence that you'll be most concerned about is the way you look. Your face is changing, just like the rest of your body. Your mouth, nose, and chin are all starting to look more like an adult's than like a child's. You'll see differences when you compare your grade-school pictures with what you see in the mirror.

When you look in that mirror, you might not always like the way your hair looks. And you may spend a lot of time trying to make it look like someone else's hair. That might work—at least until the first gust of wind.

You may go through a time when **acne**—blackheads or pimples or something more bothersome—will affect the way your face looks. Acne can be caused by overgrowth of skin, clogged pores, oil production, and bacteria, and boys are more prone to getting acne on their back. If basic cleanliness and standard acne treatments don't seem to control it, talk to your doctor about it. Acne is not a fun part of growing up, but people understand it's a common condition. They won't notice it as much as you do. And the good news is that it usually lessens or passes by the time you are eighteen or nineteen years old.

Another change you'll notice is the way you smell. Your sweat glands are starting to send out chemicals that can make sweat smell stronger. Body odor is a result of sweat and bacteria on your skin. It's important to shower daily and to wash your sports uniforms after each game or practice. Take your shoes and other equipment out of your gym bag so they can air dry when you get home. Be sure to wear deodorant or antiperspirant every day. Antiperspirants stop the sweat, and deodorants stop the smell; some products do both.

Besides body odor caused by sweating, you may start to feel more conscious about your mouth having an odor (bad breath). This is often caused by not taking good care of your teeth and gums. Prevent bad breath by brushing (including your tongue) and flossing regularly, using breath mints, and of course, avoiding cigarettes.

Although it's important to take care of your God-given body, it's also important not to dwell on your looks. Jesus reminds us that He takes care of every living thing, and we are much more important to Him than a bird or a flower. "Do not be anxious about your life, what you will eat or what you will drink, nor about your body, what you will put on. Is not . . . the body more than clothing? . . . Therefore do not be anxious about tomorrow, for tomorrow will be anxious for itself. Sufficient for the day is its own trouble" (Matthew 6:25, 34).

Growing Sexually

The **pituitary gland**, located at the bottom of your brain, regulates most of the growth changes taking place in your body. This gland also causes your sexual glands to mature. As that happens, growth usually slows down and sexual maturity is reached. These glands produces **hormones** that cause a number of changes in your body. The most obvious of these changes are those that distinguish females from males.

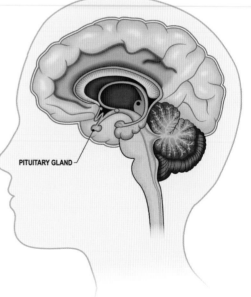

PITUITARY GLAND

You will notice that your hips will become wider and your breasts will begin to grow, perhaps as early as age 9 or 10. Hair will begin to grow under your arms, on your legs, and in your pubic area. Your voice will mature, becoming richer and fuller.

What do I most look forward to when I think about becoming a woman?

Boys generally experience the physical changes associated with puberty sometime between ages 11 and 17. A boy's chest will expand, and his shoulders will become wider. Hair will appear under his arms, on his chest, on his face, and in his pubic area. His voice, too, will change, but not as easily as does a girl's. He may find that as his voice changes when he is about 14 or 15; it will crack and squeak without warning until the change is complete. Boys may begin to shave by age 16, something they'll continue through most of their life.

Remember, these changes will occur at different times and in different ways. You may be maturing faster than most of your peers, or you may appear to be standing still. But you are changing, even if you can't see it or feel it yet.

Perhaps at times you feel embarrassed about the changes that are taking place in your body. Embarrassment can be healthy and good, a normal reaction that shows you are demonstrating proper regard for your body. God desires His people to be concerned about issues of sexual purity and modesty. Being pure has to do with not mistreating or disrespecting God's gift of sexuality. Being modest has to do with respecting God's gift of sexuality and keeping private things private, without drawing attention to yourself.

Being modest and sexually pure? Again, this is not the message you will hear from some friends or from the culture that surrounds you. This can make growing up in a godly way very difficult because you don't want to draw attention to yourself by being different. However, being committed to modesty and purity gives young Christian women and men the opportunity to show their friends something different that is truly countercultural. If our culture says it is okay to be immodest and sexually active, it is countercultural to be different from that culture.

Scripture says that we, God's people, are the "called-out ones." That means God calls us to be *set apart*—different—from a culture that doesn't know or honor Him. By being different, we are a living witness to His love, His call, for all people. God calls everyone in Christ. Many just refuse to listen. Modesty and purity are simple acts of evangelism.

At times, you're sure to get frustrated about all the changes happening in and around you, and there will be moments when others just can't seem to understand your moods and feelings. Even when your friends and parents get impatient, God understands. He has a plan for you. His patience never grows thin; He's watching and He's in control. His love continues even when you and everyone else are changing.

These thoughts and feelings are not unusual or abnormal. They are very much a part of growing up, a natural part of learning to adjust to a growing body. Some of these feelings show you need assurance; others show you need information. The chapters that follow in this book provide both. As you prepare to read and discuss them, you might find it helpful to review or add to the questions you wrote down while reading chapter 1. You may want to share the questions with a close female friend who can relate to what you are experiencing, or you may wish to keep them to yourself as you read the following chapters.

Critical Thinking:

- **What do we know about God and His love even as we face changes in our own lives and in the lives of those around us?**

- **Why is it important for you to be modest and pure?**

Remember:

- You may feel like a stranger to yourself. You may not be sure what is happening.

- You may feel embarrassed talking to others, even those your own age, especially if they're developing at a different rate than you are.

- You may feel out of place if you haven't developed as much as some of your friends have.

- You might have trouble being honest about your own feelings, even with yourself.

- You might feel pressure to conform to what others expect of you and to look and act like everyone else, even when you don't want to.

- You might find yourself wanting to be alone more than ever before.

- You might find yourself thinking more about boys, even dreaming or fantasizing about sex. You might be feeling guilty about these thoughts and the feelings that go along with them.

And as you walk the journey through this stage, remember these things:

- God loves you; He made you just the way you are.

- You need to learn to respect yourself and your body before you can start respecting other people and their bodies.

- Your parents and other adults made it through adolescence, and so will you.

7 Becoming a Woman

You are experiencing or are about to experience a unique part of God's design for you called **puberty**—the time during adolescence when you mature physically and change from a girl into a woman. You will begin to think and express yourself, work, play, and socialize as a mature female. You will relate to others—males and females—as a woman. After puberty, you will be physically capable of being a mother. If you have not already seen signs that this change is happening, you will soon.

The physical indication that a girl has become a woman begins when the **ovaries**, the female organs of reproduction located near the center of the abdomen, receive a message from the pituitary gland to begin producing the hormone estrogen. This hormone causes the girl's body to mature and change. When the ovaries mature, they begin to develop egg cells smaller than a pinpoint. Once this happens, one egg cell or **ovum** is released from the ovaries about every 28 days. This is called **ovulation**.

From the ovaries, the tiny egg moves to the nearby **fallopian tube**, which leads to the uterus or womb. If male cells are present, fertilization occurs in the tube. The fertilized

> How does a girl's body change during adolescence?

© iStock.com / Clinton Johnston

40

egg arrives in the **uterus** (or womb) in about four days. In the uterus, the egg—if it has been fertilized by a male cell—will grow to become a baby. At this moment, God has created a new life! The act of an egg cell being fertilized by a sperm cell is called conception; the fertilized cell is called a **zygote**. A human embryo is a new life from conception!

The uterus is a thick-walled, stretchy, hollow organ about the size and shape of a fist. It can expand, like a balloon, to hold a growing baby. At the lower end of the uterus is the **cervix**. The cervix opens into the **vagina**, the passageway from the uterus to the outside of the body.

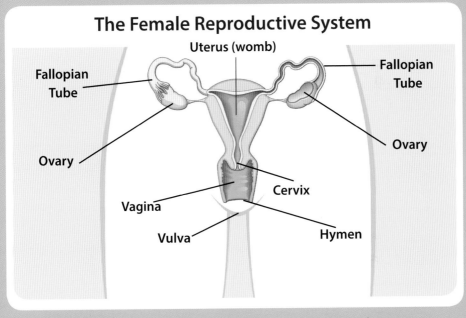

The Female Reproductive System

The outside opening of the vagina is between the legs, where it is covered by folds of skin called the **vulva**. At the top of the vulva, where the inner folds of skin meet, is the **clitoris**, a rounded tip of flesh the size of a pea.

The outside opening of the vagina in most girls is partially covered by the **hymen**, a thin membrane. This is a fringe of tissue around the opening of the vagina that will be torn the first time a woman has sex, although it could be torn before that during athletics or when inserting a **tampon**. The opening in the hymen lets blood pass through during menstruation and for the use of tampons.

The opening of the vagina lies between two other openings in the woman's body. In front is the **urethra**, from which urine leaves the body, and in back is the **anus**, from which solid waste leaves the body by way of the large intestine. Don't be embarrassed to hold a mirror beneath your vaginal area in order to better see and understand the amazing way God designed your body.

Egg cells that leave the ovaries and are not fertilized soon break up and pass from the walls of the uterus through the vagina with a combination of waste tissue and blood. This occurs about two weeks after they leave the ovaries. The process is called **menstruation**. Most girls begin to menstruate when they are age 12 or 13, but some begin to menstruate as early as 9 or as late as 16. Since the body has a regular period in which this occurs, menstruation is commonly called a woman's **period**. The normal period lasts from 3 to 7 days and occurs approximately every 28 days. The first periods are likely to be irregular and even skip a month or two before a regular cycle is established. The first period is called menarche, which means "beginning." Menstruation is not a sickness; it is the regular reminder that a woman's body is ready for motherhood when God decides it is time for fertilization to occur.

What happens when you have your period?

To protect your clothing during menstruation, you will use sanitary pads or tampons to catch the blood from the uterus. **Maxi pads** (also called sanitary napkins) are soft pads placed in your underpants; tampons are little rolls of absorbent material that you insert into the vagina. Talk to your mother, a school nurse, or a doctor if you have any questions.

When you are having your period, you may feel self-conscious and wonder if others can tell. As long as you practice good hygiene, no one needs to know. It's important to bathe or shower every day and to change your pad or tampon regularly. You will soon learn how often you need to change your pad or tampon. Consider how to discreetly carry your fresh pad or tampon to the restroom so no one notices, but remember that having your period is normal. Wrap used pads in toilet paper and put them in a waste can, never in a toilet. Tampons can be disposed of in the same way, although they can be flushed down the toilet in most new sewage systems. Some public places post signs if they prefer you throw the tampon in the trash. And remember, nearly every woman menstruates.

Because your first periods may not be very regular, you may want to wear a small, thin pad called a pantiliner when it's been a little less than a month since your last period. That may give you more confidence about realizing your period has started rather than waiting until it's too late and you're not prepared. These also need to be changed regularly, even if you're not menstruating.

When you menstruate, do whatever you usually do. Take gym class, wash your hair, and even swim (wear a tampon). Some girls have mild pains below their waist (called cramps because the muscles of the uterus are contracting) or feel a little tired and crabby during the first day or two. They may choose to take ibuprofen during that time to take any cramping pains away. Some girls might choose to cut down on active sports, but most girls will probably find that some exercise makes them feel better.

Because your body is producing hormones, you may feel moody, especially during the days right before your period. This is called pre-menstrual syndrome, or PMS. You may feel more anxious or irritable. You may even feel like eating differently. During this time, it is helpful to exercise to boost your mood. Exercise increases blood flow to the brain and sends messages to the brain to release chemicals, which make you feel better.

After the menstrual period is over, the process repeats itself. Another egg cell matures and is released about two weeks after menstruation when the follicle (the larger cell mass sheltering the growing egg) ripens. If the egg is not fertilized, menstruation again occurs. The whole series of events is called the menstrual cycle. It normally repeats itself, except during pregnancy, about every twenty-eight days until a woman is forty-five to fifty-five years old. Periods stop when a woman's ovaries no longer release egg cells.

Although the most common questions that girls your age ask are about ovulation, fertilization, and menstruation, you may have other questions about the development and maturation of your body. Perhaps you are concerned that your breasts don't seem to be developing as quickly or as fully as those of other girls your age or that you are developing too quickly or too fully. You may think it would be convenient if patterns were more consistent—that all girls' breasts started developing at exactly eleven years, for example—but that is not the way that God designed your body to develop. You have your own personal growth pattern or clock. You can be sure that you will develop at just the rate God intended for your body when He created you. That may be earlier or later than some of your friends. It will happen, and it is normal to be different.

These are the signs that show you're maturing:

- You're growing quickly.
- Your hips start to broaden.
- Your breasts may begin developing. It's not unusual for one breast to grow more rapidly than the other.
- Your pubic hair begins growing. This usually occurs before menstruation and appears in a variety of shapes and amounts.
- Your vagina may begin to produce a white or yellow discharge (something that comes out), which you may notice on your panties. Unless it is itchy, there is no need for concern. God designed your body this way to help keep your vagina clean and moist.

There you have it. The process may be awe-filled, but it is not awful. God uniquely created women for a specific purpose to complement men in society and especially within marriage.

You have a wonderful body. The more you find out about it, the more you will appreciate what God has given you. Unlike a man, you now have the potential to have a baby. Motherhood is an awesome gift with great responsibility. By God's design, you can cherish the gift of maturing into a young woman and prepare yourself to become a wife and mother.

Whether you eventually have children will depend on you, on your husband, and on God, but being a mother is only one part of being a woman. More important is how you use or control the fact that you are a woman in your relationships with others. Even though the body is beginning to be ready to create new life, girls at your age are not yet prepared emotionally or spiritually to be mothers. God designed sex to be a union between a husband and a wife who are joined not only physically and spiritually but also emotionally. Sex is not just something God gave women to feel good for a moment. When you're having sex, you're intimately sharing your body with another person. You're showing a commitment and union to that person. You're promising that you're ready to take on the responsibility of being a wife and mother.

The Bible gives a picture of what your relationship with your husband should be like, when the time comes. Jesus is the groom, and the Church (all Christians together) is the bride. A husband's love is to be self-sacrificial. A husband is willing to sacrifice his own desires and comforts for his wife and to think of his wife's needs before his own. A wife is to honor and respect her husband as the Church honors and respects Jesus. God promised the Church that He would never leave her. A husband is to remain faithful to his wife until death parts them. Marriage brings a special companionship and trust.

For women, part of living a life of love includes supporting their husbands as the spiritual leaders in society and in the home, where together they have the responsibility to bring up children "in the discipline and instruction of the Lord" (Ephesians 6:4). Through God's Word, Jesus empowers His people to "walk in love, as Christ loved us and gave Himself up for us, a fragrant offering and sacrifice to God" (Ephesians 5:2). Jesus has promised to "equip you with everything good that you may do His will, working in us that which is pleasing in His sight, through Jesus" (Hebrews 13:21). He strengthens you to serve!

When you become a woman, God's design is for you to be a blessing to the people He places in your life. Someday you may marry and be blessed with a relationship in which you love, encourage, and nurture your husband. You may bear a child, or many children, and have a special relationship in which you will raise your children in a godly home where Christlike behaviors are taught and lived. Whether or not you marry or bear children doesn't change the gift or wonder of God's plan for you as a woman. You are complete, special, important, and made in the image of God. You will be a woman, someone who lives and breathes and loves and gives. With the women of the Bible, you can celebrate your relationship with God, as Hannah said, "My heart exults in the Lord" (1 Samuel 2:1).

Critical Thinking:

- **What characteristics do you think of when you think of a "respectful" female? Do you admire women who are loving? hard-working? compassionate and caring? Over the next ten years, how will you develop the characteristics you mentioned? Develop a plan to grow in those areas.**

- **Why do you think God designed our bodies to slowly change from childhood to adulthood? Why didn't He have us change into a grownup overnight?**

8

About Boys and Men

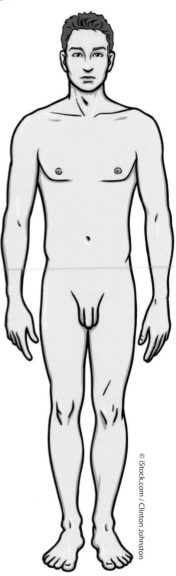

Boys may be different from girls, but they have just as many questions. The questions are slightly different, but they show many similar concerns about sex. Boys may wonder about things like this:

- **What size should a penis be?**
- **Is it wrong to have "wet dreams"?**
- **What makes me feel the way I do about sex?**

Questions like these are normal, natural, and necessary. When a boy reaches puberty, he becomes a man and is physically capable of being a father. There is even less consistency about when boys reach puberty than there is with girls. One fourteen-year-old may not yet have any sign of hair on his face, while another the same age might be 6'2" and have a beard. A foot difference in height between boys this age is not at all unusual. Boys usually reach puberty between ages 10 and 15, a year or two after girls. This fact helps explain why girls are usually far more interested in dating during junior high than are boys. But the time will come when boys will catch up, and it will come soon.

Although a man's reproductive system is less complicated than a woman's and doesn't run by a calendar, it is no less miraculous and no less interesting. The two most important parts of the man's reproductive system are the **testicles** and the **penis**. The testicles produce **sperm**, the male cell that fertilizes the female egg. They also produce the hormone testosterone, which causes boys' voices to become lower and hair to develop on their bodies at puberty. The two testicles hang behind the penis in a bag called the **scrotum**.

In order to produce sperm cells, the testicles must have a temperature that is a little lower than the temperature inside the body. The temperature must be kept constant or the sperm cells already produced will die. How did God design the scrotum and testicles to take care of these needs?

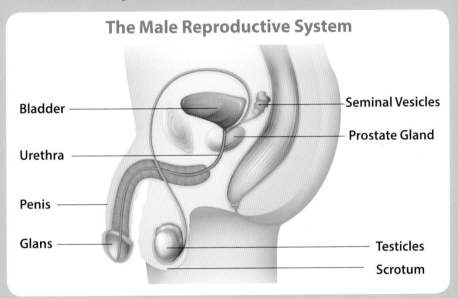

The Male Reproductive System

Bladder

Urethra

Penis

Glans

Seminal Vesicles

Prostate Gland

Testicles

Scrotum

God placed the testicles outside the body. He designed the scrotum so it automatically contracts and draws the testicles closer to the body when the outside temperature grows colder. When the body overheats, the scrotum relaxes so the testicles may be farther from the warm pelvis. So the testicles do not injure each other when body movement brings the legs close together, God designed one testicle to hang lower in the scrotum than the other. What a wonderful design God chose for man's scrotum and testicles!

What size should a penis be?

The penis hangs between the legs, in front of the testicles. It is made up of spongy tissue filled with large blood vessels. The average adult penis is three to four inches in length when it is limp, but penis size varies greatly from man to man. The size of the penis has nothing to do with a man's ability to have sexual intercourse or to become a father.

At birth, the end of the penis is partly covered by a loose skin called the **foreskin**. Some boys have this skin removed, usually just after birth, by a simple operation called **circumcision**. The reason for circumcision may be medical—the foreskin is too tight—or hygienic. Some believe it is easier to keep a circumcised penis clean.

Through the center of the penis runs the **urethra**, the tube through which both sperm cells and urine leave the body. The urethra continues inside the body, extending to the bladder, where urine is stored.

If both sperm and urine pass through the urethra, do they come out at the same time? No. God has provided a wonderful mechanism to keep the sperm and urine separate. A valve at the upper end of the urethra opens to let the urine pass out. This same valve closes tight, keeping the urine in the bladder, when sperm pass through the urethra.

The sperm, then, move from each testicle, where they are produced, up through thin tubes inside the body. These tubes—one from each testicle—are connected with the **prostate gland** at the base of the bladder. The prostate gland produces a whitish fluid in which the sperm cells swim. The sperm cells and this fluid together are called **semen**.

An **erection** of the penis occurs when the blood vessels in the penis expand to bring more blood into the penis. Valves in the vessels keep this blood under pressure, causing the spongy walls of the penis to expand and become hard. Even babies and young boys experience erections, but they are more common after a boy reaches puberty.

Sometimes erections occur from physical reasons, such as the need to urinate. Even tight clothes can cause an erection. The most common cause, though, is sexual excitement. Movement of or pressure on the erect penis, such as happens during sexual intercourse, will eventually result in an **ejaculation**, the release of semen from the penis in a series of throbbing spurts. The amount of this white, sticky fluid is one to three teaspoons. Though sperm cells are only a small part of the fluid, one ejaculation can contain as many as 400 million sperm, each capable of fertilizing a single female egg.

What's a wet dream?

Sometimes, at night, young men experience an ejaculation and wake up worried and upset. This is called a **nocturnal emission** or "wet dream," and it is perfectly normal. It is simply the body getting rid of excess semen. It first happens to most boys around age 13 to 16. Some young men have a lot of nocturnal emissions; some have few. The experience is natural and should not be thought of as abnormal or harmful.

God has given each man a wonderful body. Like a woman, a man has the potential to make a baby, although not every man will become a father. Of greater importance is how a man uses or controls the fact that he is a man in the relationships he builds with others. God made men as they are to be a blessing to others and to honor Him. It's a challenge and an opportunity to be a man. For men, part of living a life of love includes being spiritual leaders in society and in the home, where they have the responsibility to bring up children "in the discipline and instruction of the Lord" (Ephesians 6:4).

God's plan was damaged by the first sin of the first man, Adam. But we rejoice in God's plan for us through the Son of Man, Jesus, who is also true God. Romans 5:19 says that "as by the one man's disobedience the many were made sinners, so by the one man's obedience the many will be made righteous." Jesus lived in perfect obedience to God's will, died to earn our forgiveness and salvation, and rose again to demonstrate His victorious power. Jesus is a real male hero and the ultimate male role model. He sacrificed Himself to achieve our salvation. Through Word and Sacrament, His believers can "walk in love, as Christ loved us and gave Himself up for us, a fragrant offering and sacrifice to God" (Ephesians 5:2).

God made Adam, our first father, from the dust of the ground. But God fashioned Eve, the first woman, from one of Adam's ribs. When Adam saw Eve, he recognized immediately that she was just what he needed in his life. Men are attracted to women. A man recognizes and values the wholeness he experiences when he is with a woman, just as Adam did. (See Genesis 2:23.)

Men tend to be highly visual—stimulated by what they see. God designed men to appreciate the beauty of the female body, and He designed women to appreciate men as well. This appreciation is not wrong or sinful. But Satan, the world, and our sinful human nature commonly use the natural attraction men and women have for each other to entice us to sinful thoughts and actions. These sinful behaviors include viewing pornography (pictures or videos that misuse God's gift of sex) or taking part in forms of entertainment that misuse, misrepresent, or otherwise disrespect and degrade human sexuality.

God designed men and women with wonderful bodies capable of joining together as one in marriage in an act that brings new life into the world. His design is for men and women to experience this sexual intimacy only as husband and wife within marriage. God's Word is clear. He created male and female. He instituted marriage. These are God's gifts and His to give to us on His terms. Because He loves us, we can trust that this design is for our benefit.

Your body is an awesome gift, but with this gift comes the responsibility to treat it properly and respect it. You have been given this same responsibility toward the body of every other individual for whom Jesus also gave His life. Jesus showed His love for us through sacrificing Himself for our sake. "God shows His love for us in that while we were still sinners, Christ died for us" (Romans 5:8). We didn't deserve it; Jesus just loves us that much.

Jesus is God, yet He humbled Himself to become a human in order to do this. He was a servant leader, even washing the dirty feet of His disciples. Jesus calls you to follow His example and serve others too. "'A new commandment I give to you, that you love one another'" (John 13:34). As you show respect to others, serve them, and think of their needs before your own, you are showing true, self-sacrificial love.

Critical Thinking:

- **What does it mean to you that Jesus died to pay for your sins?**

- **What does that teach you about love, especially about how you will love your future husband?**

The Miracle of Birth

9

"So God created man in His own image, in the image of God He created him; male and female He created them. And God blessed them. And God said to them, 'Be fruitful and multiply and fill the earth and subdue it'" (Genesis 1:27–28).

These words from Genesis show how God made man and woman for each other. He wanted them to be happy together, and He wanted them to use their bodies to produce the children that would someday fill the earth. For this reason, He made men and women different, and He made those differences something that would cause men and women to be attracted to each other. This sexual attraction is a gift of God. Men and women are made in a way and with feelings that cause them to want to be together.

Is it wrong to notice boys?

As you grow older, you will feel this attraction more and more. You will want to be with boys—in groups or with one person. As you grow older, you will want to spend more time with boys. You may well begin to spend time with one special boy. As you get to know each other, you may fall in love and begin to look forward to marriage. Doing planned activities with a person of the other sex is called dating. Through dating, a man and a woman get to know each other. If a first date leads to a second or more dates, the two people usually enjoy being together and doing things together.

Why might courtship be better than dating?

Some Christians encourage courting rather than dating. Courting refers to actions or activities undertaken in the effort to secure a spouse. In the process of courting, couples develop romantic relationships only with those each would consider a potential spouse. Ideally, courting relationships grow out of friendships.

The man and woman who have identified character qualities they

51

desire in a godly spouse allow their relationship to grow over time as they get to know each other and each other's families. Over time, they explore and share with each other their values and beliefs about God, finances, and free-time activities. They make plans for the new life they will build together in marriage.

God's original plan was for a husband and wife to live together in a faithful commitment under His blessing. God first instituted this union for Adam and Eve before they sinned. In marriage, a man and woman build a new life together, through which they love and serve both God and each other. They work together to share God's love in their family and their community. God passes the knowledge of His grace and goodness from one generation to the next within this new family.

Is it really a problem to live together before getting married?

When a man and woman live together outside the commitment of marriage, on either a temporary or trial basis, they are showing disregard for God's will. God did not plan it that way! In marriage, a husband and wife find peace and contentment and feel emotionally healthy because they trust that their spouse loves them and wants to be committed only to him or her for his or her entire life. God instituted (established) marriage because He knew what a blessing it is to bring happiness and fulfillment to our lives.

If an unmarried man and woman try to use sex to become closer to each other or to feel good about themselves, they will be disappointed and hurt. When you are married, sex shows that you are connected and united in body and spirit to only one person. But when you are not married and have sex, you may have doubts about your relationship with that person and you may feel insecure about what the person (and others) feel about you. Instead of making you feel better or making your relationship stronger, it only makes you feel worse and weakens your relationship. There is no commitment, and that way of thinking about sex can harm your future marriage. God designed sex for husbands and wives only for a very good reason.

Another thing to consider as a Christian is what *God* desires for us in our earthly relationships. Certainly He wants us to serve and respect all people, but He gives us a clearer picture of the unique relationship in marriage. As was written earlier, God says our earthly marriages are like

Christ's relationship to the Church (all believers). What does God's love look like? Faithful. Complete. Freely given. Fruitful. These four traits are beautiful words to describe God's love and the love found in Christian marriages. We might not expect people who don't trust in God to pattern their relationships on God's love, but as Christians we don't have such an excuse. Living together apart from marriage is a very clear sign that our love is not complete. It also leaves open the possibility that one of the individuals living together may not be faithful. Without the promise made in marriage, members of a couple are still holding back part of themselves from each other. What part of Himself did Jesus keep from us on the cross? No part; He gave the total gift of Himself, His own life! This is the picture God gives to help us understand how our marriages ought to work.

You will see a great deal of uncertainty and unfaithfulness in the relationships around you as you grow. Even at this young age, you can set your mind and heart on the ways of God to prepare you for the incredible bond of marriage. If God blesses you with a husband someday, you will be ready to give all of yourself to him. Having God's plan in your heart and mind can also help you identify a man who shares these same beliefs about marriage.

There is no need to "practice" before marriage so that you will be an "expert" at having sex. God made a husband and a wife for each other so they will find delight in each other. You can trust your loving, all-knowing heavenly Father's plan for your life. What honor and respect you're showing to your future husband by waiting to only share your body with him! **Abstinence** is the term used to describe not having sex. When you abstain from sex before marriage (as God wills), you will grant your husband the wonderful gift of confidence. He will know that for you there is only him and no one else to whom you will ever compare him.

What does it mean to "abstain" from having sex?

You will have joy learning more about your husband's body and what makes him happy after you are married and have promised to be faithful to only each other for your whole lives. Being intimate with another person means that you're getting to know that person extremely closely and deeply. In a committed, lifelong marriage, you can let someone know you—all of you—and feel happy and safe with being that vulnerable. What a blessing this personal, comfortable, safe, warm, dear relationship

53

with your spouse will be! This familiarity is not something you share with other men, before or during your marriage.

Because of the special and unique relationship husband and wife enjoy in marriage, God wants only married people to engage in the close, intimate, and loving act known as **sexual intercourse**, also called "sex." "Therefore a man shall leave his father and his mother [the family where he grew up] and hold fast to his wife, and they shall become one flesh" (Genesis 2:24). Husbands and wives have a special bond together. This means they have a special relationship where they share ideas, interests, and feelings. A bond also means a special promise, or covenant, between two people that shouldn't be broken. And in marriage, as in science, a bond is an attracting force that holds things together, combining, uniting, and strengthening the two.

Research shows that this bonding process occurs whenever two people are sexually intimate. The problem comes when they are not totally committed to each other and break up. This damages a person's ability to bond to another person in the future. If this sexual bonding occurs many times, the ability to trust and feel safe is made even smaller each time. Rather than getting better at intimacy, people who have sex outside of a committed marriage get worse at finding intimacy. They are making it much harder to get and enjoy what they ultimately want and what God created them to share. It actually works in the opposite way that people think!

Sex is a very special part of marriage. It's a way for a husband and wife to show their love for each other. When a husband and wife are feeling close and loving, they find a private place to be together—usually their bedroom. They kiss and caress each other. Gradually, they become ready for intercourse. That's the way God planned it. Sex is a way to show affection.

In sexual intercourse, the husband's erect penis is put into the wife's moist vagina. The penis ejaculates semen into the wife's vagina. Both the husband and wife usually feel pleasure during sexual intercourse and feel relaxed and satisfied afterwards. Soon after ejaculation, the penis again becomes limp.

Marriage is God's plan for establishing families. A husband and wife become a family, joined together by God. Sex is a physical, emotional, and spiritual reflection of that union, commitment, and love.

A husband and wife are best friends who share companionship and similar interests and values. God blessed marriage for the procreation of children, who are to be brought up in the Lord and offer Him their praise (Genesis 1:28). A home is a wonderful, safe place to share happy times, laughter, and learning experiences and to provide support for one another during difficult times. A husband and a wife are a team, working together to create a loving, healthy home and encouraging and strengthening each other. How much more two can accomplish (Ecclesiastes 4:9)! What a support when one is feeling weak! God shows His love for us through the love of our spouse.

How do I get pregnant? Will I get pregnant each time I have sex?

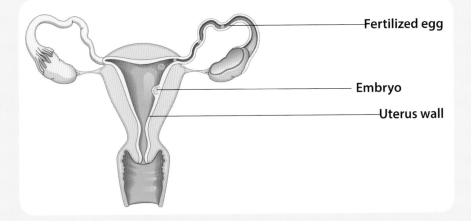

Fertilized egg

Embryo

Uterus wall

During sexual intercourse, if the woman has recently produced an egg cell, she can become pregnant. The man's sperm meet the egg cell. When one sperm enters the egg cell, that cell becomes fertilized, that is, no other sperm cell can now enter it, and that fertilized cell is the beginning of a new human being. This means the married couple has **conceived** a child. The fertilized egg gradually moves into the uterus (or womb), attaches itself to the wall of the uterus, and begins to grow. At this moment, it is smaller than a pinpoint. Until the end of the second month, it is called an **embryo**. After that, until the baby is born, the growing child is called a **fetus**, which in Latin means "young one."

Since extra blood is needed to nourish the growing egg as it develops into a baby, ovulation and menstruation do not occur while a woman is pregnant. Missing a period is one way a woman senses she might be pregnant, and it should prompt her to visit her doctor for tests that will make

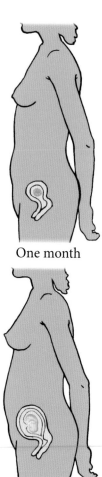

One month

sure. If the woman is pregnant, the doctor will instruct her on the best way to care for her body in order to give her baby the best chance to develop normally.

How are babies born?

About nine months after the egg and the sperm joined, the baby is ready to be born. For several months before the birth, the mother and father are able to feel their baby move in the mother's womb. Shortly before birth, the fetus usually turns in such a way that its head is pointed downward in the uterus. Then the muscles of the uterus, which have stretched to make room for the growing baby, begin to tighten and push, forcing the baby from the uterus into the vagina.

When this process, called **labor**, begins, the mother knows the birth will come soon and usually goes to the hospital so a doctor can help with the delivery. The baby usually arrives in the world headfirst from the vagina and soon gives out its first cry, a sign that it is breathing on its own. The **umbilical cord**, which joined the mother and baby in the womb and through which the baby received all its nourishment for nine months, is cut, leaving the navel, or belly button, on the baby's stomach.

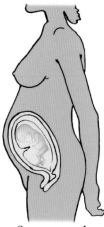

Four months

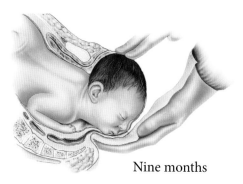

Seven months

Nine months

Following the baby's birth, the **placenta** leaves the mother's body through the vagina. The placenta is the mass of blood vessels that grew in the uterus to help provide nourishment for the baby. God's miracle of conception and birth is now complete.

After the baby is born, the mother's uterus, vagina, and vulva slowly return to their normal size. If the mother breast-feeds her new baby, her breasts grow larger and begin to produce milk. If the mother chooses to bottle-feed her child, her breasts stop producing milk and return to their normal size. The process God designed to get you from a fertilized egg to the person you are today is amazing.

Sometimes the embryo or fetus does not develop normally because of disease, injury, or some other problem. When this occurs and the baby is unable to survive or develop properly in the mother's uterus, the baby often dies and is pushed out of the body in a process called a **miscarriage**. This can be deeply painful for the mother and father who were expecting to welcome their baby into the world. It is estimated that about 10 to 20 percent of known pregnancies (the mother is aware that she is pregnant) end in miscarriage and that 30 to 50 percent of fertilized eggs are miscarried before the mother even knows she is pregnant. As brothers and sisters in Christ, we can provide comfort to the grieving parents by praying for them and sharing God's Word.

God designed it that after nine months in the uterus, babies are ready to live in the world. Babies born before they have been in the uterus nine months are called **premature babies**. They can grow to be strong and healthy, but they need extra care after they are born. They are usually kept for a while in incubators, which keep them warm and away from germs. Although it's not the way God designed it to be the most healthy, babies have been known to live if they were born at twenty-two or twenty-three weeks. Babies who have not been born yet (at first called an embryo and then at three months called a fetus) are living people; it's just best if they develop inside their mother for forty weeks.

Why do members of a family sometimes resemble one another?

"The Baby Looks Just Like You!"

Who in your family do you look like? Maybe you have your father's eyes or your mother's hair texture. Maybe you don't look very much like either of them. Maybe you were adopted, and you don't know which birth parent you look like.

Regardless, both your father and your mother passed on to you a number of the features you have.

The sperm cell from the father contains 23 tiny elements called chromosomes. Each chromosome contains hundreds of parts called **genes**, which determine what the child will look like. There are genes for the color of the skin, for the shape of the head, for body size—for all of the traits that describe how a person looks.

The egg cell of the mother also contains 23 chromosomes, each with hundreds of genes. When the father's sperm cell unites with, or fertilizes, the mother's ovum or egg cell, the fertilized cell has 46 chromosomes that determine what the new baby will look like—half of them from the mother and half from the father. Each of the father's 23 chromosomes is matched or fitted with the same chromosome of the mother. There are about 70 trillion possible combinations of chromosomes that a child could inherit!

The genes, which are the actual carriers of the features, may be either **dominant** or **recessive**. Dominant genes are stronger than recessive ones. Since genes control the way a child will look and the way the child's body will function (**heredity**), the more dominant genes will have more influence over which characteristic is reflected from parents, grandparents, and other ancestors, even though the other recessive genes act on the same trait. This helps explain why parents can have children with different colored hair than their own.

Remember, too, that both the mother and father received their chromosomes from their parents, who got them from their parents. So each newborn baby receives a good mix of characteristics from many different ancestors. That's why you may have brown eyes like your grandfather, rather than blue eyes like your mother or gray eyes like your dad.

What decided whether you're a boy or a girl? The sperm cell of the father determines the sex of the baby. There are two kinds of sperm cells. One kind has what is called an X chromosome; the other has a Y chromosome. If a sperm with an X chromosome fertilizes the ovum, the baby will be a girl. If a sperm with a Y chromosome fertilizes the egg cell, the baby will be a boy.

There are two kinds of twins, fraternal twins and identical twins. Fraternal twins begin life when two different sperm cells join two different egg cells. Fraternal twins are not much more alike than any other two children in the same family. They might be two boys, two girls, or a boy and a girl.

Identical twins begin life when one sperm cell joins one egg cell. The one new cell splits into two cells that begin to develop separately as two different people. Identical twins look exactly alike, but they are not. Each one is special. Each has his or her own interests, ideas, personalities, and experiences.

The more we study the wonders of conception and birth, the more we will agree with the psalmist: "I am . . . wonderfully made" (Psalm 139:14)!

Critical Thinking:

- Why did God create male and female? Why did He give marriage as a gift to men and women?

- Do you hope to get married someday? What are you most looking forward to for your marriage?

- How does God involve men and women in His wonderful work of creation?

Hey, Latissa, you have lots of friends, don't you?

Yeah, I guess so. Why do you ask?

I don't have very many. I mean, I wait and wait and almost nobody comes to me wanting to be my friend.

Well, you can't just sit and wait for friends to happen!

What do you mean?

Well, Ellie, you've got to be a friend to have friends.

Getting Along with Friends 10

What makes a person a friend?

Almost everyone wants to be with other people, to be liked, to be needed, to be included in groups and clubs and teams. And that's God's plan. He made people to live with and to share with other people. That's what the Church is—God's people living with, helping, and loving one another. We are a family—brothers and sisters in Christ.

If you marry someday, you will have a special person to live with and to relate to, and sex will be an important part of that relationship. But another part of being a woman is having friendships—close relationships with others—where sex is not a part of the relationship.

You and Your Friends

Being a friend and having friends is a very important part of life. Especially during your teenage years, it is important to have self-confidence and to be with others who value the gifts God has given them. Jesus said to "love your neighbor as [you love] yourself" (Mark 12:31). We also know that because God loves us, we are able to love others. Being loved by God gives you confidence. God created you with special gifts and talents, and with a unique personality. You don't have to be like everyone else to

"Liking yourself" is not a matter of pride, vanity, or conceit. Liking yourself is recognizing who you are as a daughter of our heavenly Father, the maker of the universe, whose Son gave His very life to redeem and save you. Liking yourself is appreciating the good gifts with which God has uniquely blessed you. If you find much to like about yourself, you will find there is much to like in others too.

61

find a friend. You can be confident that you will find friends who like you just the way you are, the way God created you to be. This confidence in yourself is part of being a good friend to others.

What else makes a person a good friend? Place check marks in the appropriate places on the following chart as you think about friendship and being a good friend.

A Friend . . .	I want a friend who	I see myself as a friend who
is understanding		
listens		
is pleasant to be around		
can be trusted		
can be counted on		
is open		
is helpful		
respects the interests of other friends		
is considerate		
is courteous		
has a good sense of humor		
has good manners		
is easy to talk to		

Are there other things you'd add to the list? Are some of these things unimportant to you? One way to check out how friendly you are—and also a way to work at becoming more friendly—is to use this list to examine yourself and to practice doing some of those things that you might not have been doing in your relationships with others. Being friendly, kind, and considerate to others will always be one of the best ways to get and to keep friends. If you are content with who God's shaping you to be and with what He's given you, you'll more likely be a happy person to be around. If you enjoy doing things for your friends that make them happy, they'll most likely appreciate how you reflect God's love.

Friendships are helpful in developing the values that guide what you do. You may notice that some of the things you do are modeled directly after actions of your friends. Perhaps you feel that you have to talk like your friends, dress in similar ways, and do the same kinds of activities. This is called peer pressure, or pressure from those your age, and it will be an important force in your life. No one wants to be too different; looking like your friends and doing what they do is an important part of feeling accepted and belonging to a group. On the outside, you want to look, dress, and act like everyone else. However, you shouldn't be defined by or feel that your worth comes from these outside characteristics. Your worth comes from God and from knowing that He loved you enough to die for you!

And the real you is made up of what's on the inside—your goals, attitudes, beliefs, and values. Maturity results from struggling with the influence of these two forces. Part of growing up is understanding the feeling inside of you that what you're doing or listening to or talking about isn't what pleases God, and then having the courage to stop doing it or listening to it or talking about it. The Bible says, "Do not be conformed to this world, but be transformed by the renewal of your mind, that by testing you may discern what is the will of God, what is good and acceptable and perfect" (Romans 12:2).

Most of the time, it is okay to try to be like your friends, especially if your friends hold values and moral standards similar to yours. Good Christian friends are a gift from God. Not only can they share the Gospel and encourage you when you need it, but they can also remind you when you're not living like a child of God. Friends can hold one another accountable for their actions not because they want to be bossy, but because they care. If your friend was going to do something that would hurt herself or someone else (like a wild stunt or prank), would it be better to say something even if it makes you feel uncomfortable or to be quiet and watch someone get hurt?

How are Christian friends gifts from God?

But if you feel the constant pull from your friends to do things or say things that are different from the things that you believe are right, you are likely to create tension for yourself and for your relationship with your family. You need to choose your friends wisely. If the people you spend time with smoke cigarettes, drink alcohol, use drugs, skip school, have premarital sex, or lie to parents and teachers, you're more likely to give in to those temptations as well.

God has given you rules to guide your decisions so that you won't get hurt; He wants your joy to be full, so He says to stay connected to Him (John 15:10–11). He has given you parents, teachers, pastors, and other authority figures to remind you of God's will when needed. Most often, they do this because they love you and know the consequences of poor choices.

There is a danger in drawing too much of your identity from those around you. Do you feel like you need to give in to peer pressure in order to be liked and to fit in? Do you worry that other people will make fun of you if you don't go along with what they're doing? You are a child of God, the almighty God, who fights for you, strengthens you, and protects you. You need to be secure in who you are, because at some point you will be tested to do something that doesn't go along with who you are as God's child.

What makes Jesus my truest friend?

Your best and truest friend is Jesus Himself. He knows your every thought, worry, fear, hope, and aspiration. He gave His very life to ear forgiveness for all the wrong things you have done and to grant you a home someday in heaven. He also gave you a family to love and support you here on earth and the Holy Spirit to guide you and help you understand God's will. Friends who share your love for Jesus are another special gift from God. Like your family, Christian friends support you and encourage you to live according to God's Word and to share the Good News of Jesus with others. It's a good feeling to know that family and good friends will love you through thick and thin, and that no matter what you do or don't do, Jesus will always love you.

Pornography

One of the temptations that you will have to face, possibly even from a friend, is **pornography**: pictures, writings, and videos that show or describe naked people or sex in very shameful, degrading, and even violent ways in order to cause an emotional reaction (sexual excitement). Pornography doesn't show you the beauty and wonder of sexual intimacy; rather, it creates a false sexuality and displays it in unhealthy, harmful ways.

What is pornography? Why do people look at it?

64

Pornography takes sex, a private and intimate act designed by God for husband and wife, and twists it into something public and not intimate. Pornography makes sex, the giving of yourself to the one you promise to always love, seem like something self-gratifying and self-serving. Some Internet sites, magazines, and X- and R-rated movies show the body as something to be used, abused, and lusted after rather than something to be thankful for, admired, and treated as a gift of God.

Is it wrong to look at pictures of nude people?

Most of these books, pictures, and websites claim to be off-limits to those under age 18 or 19, but junior high students may still come into contact with pornography—even though they may not be looking for it. We live in a society that glamorizes sex and bodies through ads, books, movies, TV, and the Internet. It's all around us. Be careful! You will encounter pornography, whether it's on pop-up ads, Internet searches, social media posts, or even your friends telling you about something they saw.

Pornography can easily become an addiction, so do not start viewing it thinking that you can stop. And like many addictions, it will not affect just you; it also will affect others. Not only will it hurt you now, but it will also hurt you in the future. For example, pornography does not teach you how to have "good" sex; watching or reading about another naked man makes it difficult to treat your future husband with respect, admiration, or as a gift from God to you. Pornography causes emotional pain because the sex depicted there is not real and may create unreasonable expectations for you and your future husband, leaving you to feel inadequate.

It will not be an easy temptation for you to ignore, but there are things you can do. You can always remember that the Holy Spirit gives you power to resist temptation and to exercise self-control. Remember that your body and the bodies of others are the gifts of God. You can be aware that such pornographic materials exist, yet you can avoid them. You can avoid those situations with people whose actions and words degrade sex and the human body. You can seek the support and encouragement of other young people who share your love of Jesus and desire to live for Him. You can pray daily for strength to resist the pressure to conform. (See Romans 12:2.) You can take care not to tell improper stories regarding sexually explicit acts or to wear revealing clothing that may tempt others to think impure thoughts.

Masturbation

Is masturbating wrong?

Another thing you might hear your friends talking about is masturbation. **Masturbation** involves the handling or rubbing of the clitoris or penis to gain pleasure or until release of sexual pressure, or **orgasm**, is reached.

God designed sex to be a wonderful experience for husband and wife. They experience a sense of peace and satisfaction after sex. There seems to be evidence that having an orgasm (sexual release) is a form of stress relief, a natural sleep sedative, and a mood booster through the release of endorphins. These same chemicals are also released during masturbation, allowing some of the benefits of sexual intimacy to be had in a self-serving way. However, the release of these powerful neurochemicals makes stopping the habit of masturbation difficult. It can easily become a compulsion or (chemical) addiction! It may start to occupy a person's thoughts and interfere with her daily activities, schedule, and relationships.

More important, masturbation is not God's intention for our use of the gift of sex because God intended that our sexual activity be directed toward communion with another person in the mutual love and commitment of marriage. Masturbation separates sexual satisfaction from the giving and receiving of sex in the union of marriage.

Young women need to consider the lasting effects of masturbation instead of thinking of their desires at the moment. While masturbating, a person might have thoughts about a boy that may later make her feel ashamed or guilty. She may feel guilty about masturbation and may fear getting caught. These emotions may continue to affect a person after she is married. God's Word says that as a child grows and matures, youthful lusts and fantasies are to be left behind (2 Timothy 2:22).

It is believed that stress, fear, and guilt caused by masturbation can play a role in **premature (early) ejaculation** by men. This means that males reach an orgasm (climax) and ejaculate earlier than they and their partner would like, which decreases the length of time they are able to enjoy time with their partner during the act of sex. If a male is in a hurry to reach a climax during masturbation when he is young, it may condition his body for premature ejaculation in adulthood. Thirty to seventy percent of males younger than age 40 have been or are affected to some degree by premature ejaculation.

Masturbation can also impact marriage later because it allows a young woman to train her sexual desires to be self-centered, rather than focused on her spouse and their relationship together. This way of thinking can cause conflict later in relationships and could even lead to a wife preferring masturbation over having sex with her husband.

It is likely that you have encountered messages that say masturbation is okay. It is important to note that much of this type of approval comes from people who have no relationship with God through Jesus Christ. You must ask yourself if masturbation is God's will for you and whether it reflects the kind of love He has for us. You must also be careful to not assign greater weight to masturbation than is warranted. Some people feel so consumed by guilt that they think God could never forgive them. Of course, that's not true. It is best to understand that masturbation is a behavior that can turn us away from God's plan for our lives, but also that He freely loves us and forgives our sins.

Here are some ways to overcome the habit of masturbation: spend more time in activities with others—sports, clubs, hobbies—whatever interests you and will bring you into contact with people. Exercise also releases endorphins that boost your mood. By sharing God's love through acts of service and volunteerism, you will find a sense of satisfaction and love. It's rewarding to do things for other people.

Avoid pictures, books, magazines, websites, and conversations that are sexually stimulating. "Whatever is true . . . whatever is pure, whatever is lovely . . . think about these things," writes the apostle Paul (Philippians 4:8). In other words, enjoy activities, music, books, parks, funny people, worship, Bible study, cooking, and projects where the focus is on friendship and fellowship and not on sex. If you really think about it, the act of sex is just a tiny fraction of all the time in our lives that is spent doing other things. It really isn't all about sex!

Most of all, ask God for His strength and power to resist temptation. "No temptation has overtaken you that is not common to man. God is faithful, and He will not let you be tempted beyond your ability, but with the temptation He will also provide the way of escape, that you may be able to endure it" (1 Corinthians 10:13). Trust that the Holy Spirit dwelling in you will give you self-control (Galatians 5:23).

Should I have only Christian friends?

And remember that no matter what mistakes you've made or unhealthy thoughts you've had, God keeps on loving you and forgiving you for Jesus' sake. Jesus has taken our sins away—completely, forever. If you feel overwhelmed about stopping sinful habits, remember that Jesus changes our lives and makes us new through His power. Each day, He makes us new and frees us from the hold sin has on us. Masturbation is another example of our human tendency to turn in upon ourselves for the satisfaction of our desires. Look to God to satisfy you with every good thing that you need (Psalm 145:15–17). He brings you true, lasting fulfillment and peace.

You should not avoid contact with those people who believe and live differently than you. Instead, you can be a Christian example for them. You can share the Good News of God's love and forgiveness, even with those who laugh at you for being a Christian. God works in you so that "you may be blameless and innocent, children of God without blemish in the midst of a crooked and twisted generation, among whom you shine as lights in the world" (Philippians 2:15). People who don't follow God's ways are walking in darkness. Your faith in Christ becomes a light to them that draws them to Christ and His Word of salvation.

Look for ways to reach out and broaden your circle of friends. Not only will you have opportunities to share your faith, but you will also have more of an opportunity to appreciate the diversity of people God created. We serve other people in kindness and love, no matter what their faith.

You can be friendly to everybody. A happy smile, a cheerful "hi," can go a long way in helping people see you as a friendly person. It's pretty hard for anyone to ignore that kind of greeting, and it is a good way to invite others to want to find out more about you. God has given you many, many blessings, especially forgiveness and eternal life. Thinking about what you're thankful for is sure to put a smile on your face.

Critical Thinking:

- If you regularly, secretly masturbate to quickly reach an orgasm, what are your body and mind learning that may affect your sexual intimacy in marriage?

- Why are Christian friends important? How can you best serve friends who may not know or believe in Jesus?

What about Dating and Hooking Up?

11

Even if you've never had a date, you've probably thought about dating. Dating is generally defined as meeting with someone you feel is attractive, physically and because of her personality.. The purpose of dating is to do an activity together, get to know the other person better, and enjoy companionship. Today, if a male and a female are dating, it typically means they are in an exclusive relationship. **Hooking up**, on the other hand, does not imply there is or will be any relationship between the two people. The purpose of hooking up is to make out or have sex.

In the years ahead, the pressure increases to date and to talk about dating. Even if you're not particularly excited about dating now, it won't hurt to think about it and to talk about the reasons teenagers want to date.

These are some of the more common reasons why teens date:

1. You don't want to be alone.

2. You want to feel accepted and worthwhile.

3. Some of your friends are dating.

4. You need to feel independent, to move away from family influence and be on your own.

5. You want a chance to try out adult behavior.

6. You want to develop close relationships with young men.

7. You want the special feeling that comes when someone cares enough for you to want to be with you.

No doubt you can add other reasons for wanting to date, but maybe your present thoughts about dating are more in the form of questions. Maybe you have some questions like these:

1. How old should I be before I start dating? Is it wrong not to want to date yet?

2. How can I show my affection toward a boy on a date without giving him the wrong idea?

3. Is it okay for me to ask a boy out? How do I get a boy to ask me out?

4. What do I do on a date?

5. What commitment am I making to the boy I go with on a date? What expectations will the boy I date have of me?

All of these are good questions and very normal ones for people your age. When you ask them, you are going to find that lots of people have answers for you. You will have some of your own answers, your friends will have some answers, and your parents and other adults are bound to want to get a few of their answers in too.

It's possible that your parents' answers will be different from your own. And that could cause conflict. Your parents will probably have some set ideas about dating—even rules or at least guidelines for dating. That's because they want the best for you.

It may not seem like it at the time, but they're really thinking of you and your interests. God holds them responsible for bringing you up as a loving, responsible Christian person. He calls on you to love, honor, and respect them. The best way to handle the conflicts that arise is to talk openly about differences without arguing. Perhaps if you accept their rules without arguing, adjustments can be made as time goes on to allow for the maturity you've shown.

Saying to your parents "everyone else can" may be true, but it probably won't help. It might be more successful to ask for special permission to stay out late for a special occasion than to push for blanket approval of a time they aren't comfortable with. Each situation will be different, though, and the best way always is to work with your parents in understanding and love.

Most of the questions about dating can't be answered in some simple, standard way for everyone. God made you different from your friends, and your development will be different from theirs in many ways. You don't have to be like everyone else in the way you feel about dating, when you start dating, or even in what you do on a date.

Keeping that in mind, here are some answers to our earlier questions that can serve as guidelines as you and your parents come up with answers that work for you.

1. **How old should I be before I start dating? Is it wrong not to want to date yet?** There's no rule about when to start dating. You don't have to prove anything to anyone by dating if you don't feel like it. But you'll want to spend time with larger groups of people, both boys and girls, doing things you like to do. Show your interest in others and in their activities. Let your own interests grow. And if special interests develop in one or more boys, fine. Participating in planned activities involving peers of both sexes is fine at any age. These activities may include things like a party, a school social, a volleyball game at the beach, a softball game in the park, or the like. No one is paired off with another specific person in this type of date, but boys and girls are getting to know one another better.

As you get to know what interests certain boys through a date with a group, you will be preparing yourself for a special kind of group date: two or three boys asking two or three girls to a party at school, church, or in the neighborhood. This kind of "double dating," in turn, will help you feel more confident and will prepare you for single dating (just one couple together) later.

Discuss with your parents whether you're ready yet for double dating—and discuss single dating too, which most young people don't begin until the high school years. And remember: just because "everyone" is dating, it doesn't mean you have to. If you are feeling satisfied and fulfilled by the activities you are involved in, and if you are already getting plenty of time interacting with boys through those activities, there is no need to "force" any romantic agenda.

Jesus brings fulfillment to your life that having a romantic relationship with a boy never can. Jesus is the one who gives you confidence because you were worth dying for. Jesus wants you to be with Him forever, and He gives that to you through faith in Him. Although it's good to think about how your relationships now can prepare you for your future relationship with

Don't I NEED a boyfriend?

your spouse, there is no need to invest your time and emotions so intently on the pursuit of "getting a boyfriend" that your spiritual, physical, or emotional health suffers. No human relationship can match God's level of commitment and love.

2. **How can I show my affection toward a boy on a date without giving him the wrong idea?** Be polite and respectful. Show the boy that you appreciate him for who he is; do not go on a date with a boy you find only physically attractive.

Dating needs to be entered into with caution and discernment. It is important not to think only of "what's in it for me?" A dating relationship should not have a self-centered approach. Likewise, consider whether the person you are doing something with is someone you could imagine yourself with on another date. Dating one boy after another will only hurt your own emotional well-being and that of the boys you have stopped dating. On the other hand, if you invest too deeply or quickly into a relationship (physically and/or emotionally), you can also feel emotionally hurt when the relationship ends.

Read what we say in this chapter under "Sexual Experimentation" and in chapter 10 about "Peer Pressure." In a hookup, it is usually the man who initiates sex. However, young women, too, should avoid trying to see what they can get out of their date. Such an approach is selfish. It conveys little respect for the other person on the date. Disrespecting another person also disrespects God and His will for His people.

Hooking up is not God's will for healthy relationships. Most hookups do not lead to a relationship. Hookups avoid the work of a real relationship. They are a quick substitute for dating or courtship, and they only hurt, complicate, and confuse the people involved. Hooking up is a selfish way to live for the moment, and it will not lead to any emotional fulfillment or satisfaction. It involves using someone as a friend with benefits and not making that person feel special or worthwhile.

What's wrong with hooking up?

Avoid situations that increase temptations. Pray for God's Spirit to guide you. Remember God's command—and the good reasons He has for restricting sex to marriage. Remember how much Christ loves you and your date—and that He gave Himself up for you on the cross!

3. **Is it okay for me to ask a boy out? How do I get a boy to ask me out?** If your parents approve of a boy/girl party and will be on hand to chaperone, plan one and invite the boy you're interested in. Or simply invite him to a social event you think he might enjoy. Ask him early and give him all the facts: when, where, and what the event is all about.

If you want a boy to ask you out, be friendly to him whenever you see him. Show you're interested in him. Whenever you see him, encourage him to talk about his activities—hobbies, schoolwork, athletic events. Try not to be too pushy. Many people shy away from others who try to take charge or who quite obviously hint that they want to be asked out.

4. **What do I do on a date?** Even when you're ready to date and want to, it's not always easy to start. You're nervous about accepting, or you're nervous about asking. You want to say and do just the right thing. Be yourself. God made you a unique person. Don't try to overdo the date, but settle for the easy things—a movie, a trip to the mall, a party of some kind. Being with another couple or two or in a group lessens the chance for awkward times when you don't know what to say and reduces the temptation to go past the boundaries of proper action that you have set.

5. **What commitment am I making to the boy I go with on a date? What expectations will the boy I date have of me?** Remember that the purpose of dating is to help you get to know and relate to boys. Whether the date is with a group or with just one boy, remember to respect yourself and all others as persons for whom Jesus died. Because you are God's child through faith, you can evidence His presence in your life in the words you speak and the things you do. Going with a boy on a date does not obligate you to any other commitments involving him.

Some Christian young people make a list of qualities they desire in a future spouse and focus on dating only people with those qualities. Courting refers to actions or activities undertaken in the effort to find a lifelong spouse. In the process of courting, couples develop romantic relationships only with those each would consider a potential spouse.

Sexual Experimentation

Maybe you've heard friends brag about experiences with making out or sex. For many, these stories are like a game or contest. Each person wants to show she knows more or is more mature and sophisticated than anyone else in the group. These stories are usually exaggerations or lies. But they can lead you to feel inferior, abnormal, or at least different from your friends. This pressure from peers may cause you to give up on your desire, and God's will, for sexual purity and prompt you to experiment with sex to prove something to others that you will later regret.

Certainly as you begin to develop a serious dating relationship, you will find that you want to kiss, hold, and touch the boy you are with. Such activities are not wrong, but you will soon discover the need to draw some lines in your own mind about what is right. Discuss with your boyfriend your boundaries and the level of respect you expect.

Where do I draw the line?

To do something just to see if you can get away with it, or to see how far you can go, degrades the person you are with. It won't lead to friendship or to real love. If you want to do something to prove your courage or so you can brag about it, you are being selfish and hurting the person you have chosen to date.

Some young people engage in oral sex, the stimulation of another's sex organs by mouth, believing that they are not engaging in sex because they are not having sexual intercourse. But oral sex and other activities of a sexual nature substitute for the type of sexual intimacy reserved for a man and woman within marriage. These activities go against God's desire for His children to remain sexually pure.

The best guideline seems to be drawing the line at those touches that might lead you and your partner beyond the point of control and into sexual intercourse. If you avoid situations that increase the chances of stepping beyond the line you have drawn, you will better enjoy your relationship. You will respect yourself and the person you are with. For example, don't get together in a house where no adults are home. Love without a permanent commitment is pretty shallow. Our love for other people is based on God's love for us; thus, all our interactions with others ought to strive to model that love, with the help of God.

Most of all, remember that as a Christian you can call on the power of God's Spirit. "Walk by the Spirit, and you will not gratify the desires of the flesh. . . . The works of the flesh are evident: sexual immorality, impurity, sensuality . . . and things like these. . . . But the fruit of the Spirit is love, joy, . . . self-control. . . . If we live by the Spirit, let us also keep in step with the Spirit" (Galatians 5:16, 19, 21–22, 23, 25).

Sexting

Sexting occurs when a person sends sexually explicit messages or images on his or her phone or other device. Popular culture would have us accept the notion that sexting is a normal part of dating and hooking up. But this type of conversation is not how we walk by the Spirit. It is also a serious violation of the law and has led some teenagers to be arrested for creating and distributing child pornography.

Although the body is a wonderful gift of God to be admired, sexting degrades the body, treating it as a sexual object for personal gratification. Sexting does not promote healthy conversation and communication. A relationship that centers around physical attraction and lust will not last and will only lead to emotional pain. Again, as with any sexual temptation, it is best to keep in mind what God's Word says: "Whatever is true . . . whatever is pure, whatever is lovely, . . . think about these things" (Philippians 4:8). Tell the person that you don't feel comfortable with the conversation, and switch the subject. If the person continues sexting, do not reply to the inappropriate texts and block the caller, if necessary.

Recreational Sex

Our culture, the media, and maybe even our friends would have us accept the notion that sex outside of marriage is a normal, healthy, even expected part of the teenage years and adulthood. In addition to the influences of the world around us, the devil would have us go along with this perspective, which also appeals to our natural inclinations because they are contaminated by sin. These forces—the world, the devil, and our sinful nature—work to lead us into sexual sin.

Sexual immorality, which includes sex outside of marriage and all misuses of God's gift of sex, disobeys the will of our Father in heaven, who desires only what is best for us. And it does have harmful consequences. Taking part in intimate sexual activity outside of marriage negatively influences your attitude about yourself and others. As Paul says, "Flee from sexual immorality. Every other sin a person commits is outside the body, but the sexually immoral person sins against his own body. Or do you not know that your body is a temple of the Holy Spirit within you, whom you have from God? You are not your own, for you were bought with a price. So glorify God in your body" (1 Corinthians 6:18–20).

Why is sex sinful before marriage but good and even commanded within marriage? God designed sex to be the highest expression of love between a husband and a wife. Sexual intercourse in marriage unites a husband and wife into "one flesh." Misuse of God's gift of sex negatively influences how we think of and treat others as well as how we regard ourselves.

Doesn't almost everyone live together before they get married?

The Bible warns against fornication and adultery. **Fornication** is sexual intercourse between unmarried people. **Adultery** is sexual intercourse by a married person with someone other than his or her spouse. In both of these sins, the man or woman gives in to his or her own selfish desires and disregards God's Law. By remaining a **virgin** (one who has not had sex) until you are married, you are obeying God's Law and staying open to all the blessings He wants to give you.

Many people who give in to these sins, of course, claim that they can love the person they are having sex with even though they are not married to that person. But what kind of love is it that says, "My pleasure comes first. I don't care what God says or what may happen if I hurt my husband by having sex with someone else"? That is not love; it is lust.

When Jesus spoke in Matthew 5:28 about a "lustful" look and "adultery" in the heart, He wasn't talking about our good, God-created interest in and attraction to people of the other sex. He meant the selfish misuse of that desire. Love cares about the other person. Lust uses the other person for its own pleasure.

"Husbands, love your wives, as Christ loved the church and gave Himself up for her" (Ephesians 5:25). Remember how Christ loves you! That's the way husbands, wives, and young people who are about to date can turn from lust and grow in love.

Birth Control

What is birth control? It is any method that people who are having intercourse use to prevent pregnancy. There are a number of birth control methods, but only one can guarantee a woman will not become pregnant. This is abstinence, or not having sex. The **birth control** methods outlined below can only reduce the chance of pregnancy, not eliminate it.

1. IUDs (or intrauterine devices) are small, T-shaped devices placed inside the uterus by a doctor. Depending on the type, they stay in the uterus for five to ten years.

2. Birth control pills, when taken regularly by a woman, prevent ovulation by making her body "think" pregnancy has taken place. Approximately one out of eleven women currently using the birth control pill will become pregnant in a year.

3. An implant is a thin rod that is inserted under the skin of a woman's upper arm. Over three years, it continuously releases a hormone to prevent pregnancy.

4. A birth control shot can be given every three months. Approximately one out of seventeen women currently getting the shot will become pregnant in a year.

5. A birth control patch can be worn on the skin. A new one is placed each week, except the fourth week so the woman can have her period. Approximately one out of ten women currently wearing a patch will become pregnant in a year.

6. A birth control ring can be placed inside the vagina for three weeks, and then removed the fourth week so the woman can have her period. Approximately one out of ten women currently wearing a ring will become pregnant in a year.

7. A contraceptive sponge is a donut-shaped barrier placed into the vagina that kills sperm. About one out of nine women currently using the sponge will become pregnant in a year.

8. Spermicides are foams, gels, creams, or tablets that are placed inside the vagina before sex to kill sperm. Between one in three and one in four women currently using spermicides will become pregnant in a year.

9. In natural methods of family planning, a woman closely keeps track of her monthly periods and her ovulation cycles. She observes changes in her cervical mucus and better identifies peak times of fertility. Thus, she learns when it is likely that fertilization, and pregnancy, may or may not occur. This method is called natural family planning, or NFP.

10. A diaphragm is a cap that a woman inserts into her vagina to keep the sperm from getting into her uterus.

11. Condoms fit over the penis and prevent the sperm from entering the vagina. Approximately one out of six women whose partner currently uses a condom will become pregnant in a year. There is also a female condom. Approximately one out of five women currently using a female condom will become pregnant in a year. Condoms are the only form of birth control that will help protect against some sexually transmitted diseases (STDs, discussed later in this chapter). However, condoms do not help protect against HPV, one of the most common types of STD.

12. Men and women also may be sterilized by having an operation that prevents pregnancy. On a man, this is done by cutting the tubes that carry sperm from the testicles. On a woman, it's done by tying shut the fallopian tubes. Both of these sterilization operations are usually permanent. They do not, however, affect the ability to have sexual intercourse.

Many Christians are concerned about the motives for practicing birth control, particularly if the couple does not want children and the responsibilities that children bring. God did bless marriage for the procreation of children (Genesis 1:28). Some Christian churches permit only "natural methods" of birth control, since they view other methods as being against God's will. They feel God determines when or if they should have a child. Another major concern for Christians is that some contraceptives aggressively attack the sperm and egg even after fertilization—after a life has been created!

Birth control allows a married couple to plan more carefully when to have children and how many they will have. Because birth control methods are readily available and to a certain extent remove the fear of pregnancy, they have no doubt encouraged more unmarried people to have sex. But why are there still pregnancies outside of marriage? For one thing, many unmarried people simply don't bother to use any birth control methods. Also, none of the birth control methods are 100 percent effective. Many have a failure rate of around 20 percent, which means that twenty out of one hundred women will experience an unintended pregnancy within a year. In our society, we frequently hear the term "**safe sex**" when contraception is discussed, but because of the failure rate of many methods, not having sex is the only truly safe method of birth control. Abstinence is the only birth control method that is 100-percent effective. That's the way God planned it!

Abstinence means reserving intimate sexual activity for marriage. Since God's Word forbids intimate sexual activity outside of marriage, obedience to God involves waiting until marriage for sexual intimacy. Waiting is especially difficult with so much pressure on young people to have sex. But God does not leave us alone to face these struggles and temptations. He strengthens and encourages us through His Word, offering to us the same power that enabled Joseph to abstain and resist the seductive pleadings of Potiphar's wife (see Genesis 39).

Unmarried—and Pregnant

There are more birth control devices than ever before, and people can get them more easily. Yet more unmarried girls are getting pregnant— even those from Christian homes. Very likely, you know of girls and boys who are experiencing or who have experienced this very real problem. It is a problem in which both girls and boys are equally involved, because it takes a boy to get a girl pregnant. In the United States, 10 percent of all births are from mothers younger than 19.

The young girl who becomes pregnant faces several decisions about what to do. She and the father of the child may decide to marry. If they do, they need to be aware of the difficulties they will face. For example, marriage at a young age has two to three times greater chance of ending in divorce than do other marriages. It can also interrupt or stop the couple from finishing school and developing their abilities. Nevertheless, such a marriage can succeed if both father and mother are willing to make the necessary sacrifices. As they trust in God for forgiveness and for strength, they can grow in their love for each other and their child.

The girl also may decide to have the baby, but then place the baby for adoption. Many girls choose to do this, letting the baby be placed in a home with parents who are able to provide for the baby in a family. A mother and father who make the sacrifice of giving up their child—and the child who is adopted by loving parents—will find special meaning in this word from God: "God sent forth His Son, born of woman, . . . so that we might receive adoption as sons. And because you are sons, God has sent the Spirit of His Son into our hearts, crying, 'Abba! Father!'" (Galatians 4:4–6).

Unfortunately, some women who are pregnant choose to have **abortions**—that is, to have their unborn baby (embryo or fetus) killed in their womb before it is born. In the United States, 22 percent of all pregnancies end in abortion. In 2011, there were over one million abortions in the U.S. Often, the cost of the abortion is paid by the father of the child. Abortion is a terrible sin! Only God has the right to give and take away life. Killing an embryo or fetus is killing a human person.

Some girls decide to have the baby and to raise it, perhaps with the help of their parents and with the financial assistance of the child's father. The mother may find it hard to take care of her baby and also continue going to school. It may be more difficult for her to get married later. But this choice saves a life. Although it's unfortunate that having sex before marriage was chosen, having the baby prevents another bad choice—an abortion—that doesn't follow God's will from happening. Keeping and raising the baby can work out as the mother looks to our Father in heaven for the support and strength she will need.

In any case, all those involved in an unplanned pregnancy need the strong support and forgiving love of relatives and friends. Most of them recognize their sin, and they need to hear God's forgiveness in Christ. They need help, too, to seek out God's will for their lives and for the baby who will be born. Regardless of the circumstances associated with any baby's birth, each individual is loved by God and redeemed by His Son.

Sexually Transmitted Diseases

What are sexually transmitted diseases (STDs)? STDs are diseases you get from having sexual intimacy with an infected person. There are many different and dangerous STDs. The most common are chlamydia, herpes, syphilis, human papilloma virus (HPV), gonorrhea, trichomoniasis, and HIV/AIDS. Doctors are researching how to cure these diseases, yet more people are getting them. STDs infect millions of teenagers each year.

The chlamydia bacterium infects the urethra in men and women and may inflame or scar the sex organs so the person becomes infertile (unable to have babies).

The herpes simplex virus (Type 2,) called genital herpes, causes itching and painful blisters on the genitals.

Signs of syphilis first appear ten to ninety days after infection as a chancre sore on or near the sex organs, but such sores don't always occur.

HPV causes warts on both women's and men's genitals and also cancer of the cervix. Because of the growing number of people having sex outside of marriage, it is estimated that nearly all sexually active people will be infected with HPV at some point in their lives. There is a vaccine available to help prevent the spread of HPV, but for Christians, abstinence from sex outside of marriage is the God-pleasing method of prevention. A husband and wife who remained sexually pure prior to marriage, despite the temptations, are sure to share a life free from STDs.

Symptoms are not always noticeable in gonorrhea, although infected men sometimes notice a whitish discharge from the penis three to eight days after infection. Women usually have no early signs that they have gonorrhea, but the later effects of the disease are as serious for them as they are for men.

Symptoms of trichomoniasis include a whitish discharge and itching, although most men have no symptoms. There is a link between trich and cervical cancer and premature delivery of babies.

Many sexually transmitted diseases can be treated and cured by early diagnosis and medical treatment. But because the diseases may not give early warning signs, many people don't know they have these diseases and so are left untreated. If they aren't treated, chlamydia, syphilis, HPV, and gonorrhea are extremely serious. They can lead to blindness, heart trouble, infertility, cancer, and even death. Although herpes is not life-threatening for most people, there is no cure; it is a disease for life. Genital warts can be treated, but there is no cure for HPV.

In 1981, doctors began to report a new disease called HIV/AIDS, a virus that can be passed from one person to another mostly by sexual contact or by sharing drug needles and syringes. This disease attacks a person's immune system and damages one's ability to fight other diseases. The body can then easily get all other life-threatening diseases, such as pneumonia, meningitis, and cancer. There is no cure for HIV/AIDS and no vaccine to prevent it.

Many HIV/AIDS patients do not get the disease through sex. Some get it from sharing infected needles when injecting themselves with illegal drugs. Others become infected through contaminated blood products. Some are born with it, because an infected mother can pass HIV/AIDS to her child in the womb and later through her breast milk. Nevertheless, the great majority of HIV/AIDS patients get the disease from sexual contact. It can take up to six months to test positive for the HIV virus and then another ten to fifteen years for symptoms to appear.

Chlamydia, herpes, syphilis, HPV, and gonorrhea come mainly from sexual contact. To prevent them, refrain from sex outside of marriage and stay faithful within marriage. If you ever have any fear that you might have such a disease, see a doctor immediately.

As you grow to be a woman, there will be times of doubt and disappointment, times of frustration, and maybe even times bordering on despair. God had a good reason for making the years of physical growth and the years of social growth happen at the same time. When they're finished, you'll feel ready to be an adult. You will learn a lot about yourself, other people, and how to have an adult relationship that is God-pleasing. Relationships take time to develop. A one-night stand will not teach you anything about marriage, because marriage is so much more than just having sex. God designed sex to be a reflection of your love for another person, not something that happens before you get to know someone. Healthy dating or courting relationships will give you great experience in communicating with others, resolving conflicts, and forgiving others. Relationships can bring much joy and fulfillment because someone else is showing you that you are special.

But our true value and fulfillment comes in knowing that we are a child of God, a brother or sister in Christ. Meaningful relationships, even having a husband someday, is something most young women desire, but our confidence is always found through our faith in Jesus, who will always be with us, always be faithful to us, and always love us unconditionally.

Critical Thinking:

- Why might your parents have different ideas about dating than you?

- What is the purpose of dating? How can you witness to your faith during your dating years?

- If sex means that you are united in body and spirit to that person, then what message are you sending if you have sex with several different people?

- What is God's plan for sexual intercourse? What are some other reasons not to have sex before you are married?

Joannie, do you like your family?

Sure. I mean, I guess so. But we do our share of arguing and fighting.

So do we. But we still love each other!

We do too. I just wish we would listen more to each other.

That's the trouble with parents, I think. They just don't listen.

Hmmm . . . that's what my parents say about ME!

Getting Along with Family

12

You may have noticed that the amount of disagreement between you and others in your family has increased in the last couple of years. Such conflict certainly isn't pleasant, but it might help to realize that it's pretty common in most families. It doesn't automatically mean that your home is falling apart or that everyone is failing in their efforts to be a family. It probably does mean that both parents and children are adjusting to new roles. If everyone sees that it is part of development, these moments of conflict can teach both parents and children to understand and to better handle these new roles.

How do I get my parents to listen to me?

This process can be difficult. You've already read about the problems that arise about matters of sex, about growing up, and about dating. And you surely can think of other areas where you or your friends have really run into trouble with parents. Whether you consider the things you argue about big things or little things, one of the biggest causes of misunderstanding is the unwillingness of either side to really listen to what the other is saying. Parent and child both feel so strongly about their position that neither one wants to consider the possibility of another point of view.

Taking time to listen to the other person will help, and so will stopping to ask why you're getting so upset. Is it really worth it? Why is it so important to you and to the other person? Instead of trying to decide who is right and who is wrong, have your discussions in love and understanding. Say a prayer for guidance, self-control, and patience at the time when an argument starts, before words and actions occur that you'll wish later you could take back.

Obviously, you're never going to be able to do everything your parents expect you to, even if you wanted to. Your parents may also disappoint you in the way they talk or act. God's plan for you and the members of your family is that each of you is willing to forgive, share, grow, and learn together in love.

Unconditional love is the kind of love Jesus shows. No matter who the person is or what the person has done, Jesus forgives. Families can have that kind of love too. Despite disagreements, conflicts, or even fighting, parents and children can still show love. The relationships in your family are important enough to continue to develop and strengthen. Forgiveness is the answer for how relationships can be mended. Despite disagreements, the home can be a happy and safe place to discuss problems and questions. God's Word reminds us, "Be angry and do not sin; do not let the sun go down on your anger" (Ephesians 4:26). In other words, forgive as Christ has forgiven you!

Sometimes parents really don't understand that you are capable of handling more responsibility; sometimes they simply expect too much. Perhaps you sometimes forget that your parents do most of what they do because they love you and want only what is best for you. It can be hard for parents to let go of the child whom they have raised and cared for in both good and bad times. Sometimes your growing up only reminds them that they are growing old. Both sides can learn a lot about patience, understanding, and sharing the love and forgiveness that God's love makes possible. His presence during all arguments can take away a lot of the sting.

Why won't my parents leave me alone?

All this understanding won't take away the areas of conflict. They will still be there. Parents may continue to remind you what they did or didn't have when they were young. They may try to shape you into something they wanted to be but didn't get to be. Maybe they'll push you toward a profession they like but in which you have no interest.

Parents will continue to want a voice in your selection of friends—of either sex. But if you listen and try to understand what they are saying, you just may hear a little wisdom and a lot of love and understanding tucked around those words that *seem* to criticize everything you do. And often, parents can be right!

You may be growing up in a single-parent home. The number of such homes is increasing and brings special needs and opportunities for teenagers. Managing such homes is especially hard for single parents, and they may expect you to carry more of the load and perhaps to grow up faster than you would need to in a two-parent home. At times, you may experience feelings of insecurity as you wonder where exactly you fit within the changing configuration of your family. It's not easy, but it's the kind of situation in which God has promised to supply a special measure of His Spirit.

Whatever your home environment, whether you live with one parent, two parents, or foster parents and whether you have younger brothers and sisters who torment you or older brothers and sisters to whom you constantly get compared, your family is God's gift to you, and you are God's gift to your family. You'll have times when you'd like to give your family back, and probably there will be times when they'd like to give you back. But your family is God's plan, His design, and He is right there with you and your family, guiding and strengthening you with His Word.

Critical Thinking:

- Why do you think teens and their parents have conflict?

- Why should parents and children take time to listen to one another? Why is it important to always be ready to forgive?

- What difference can God's love and forgiveness make in day-to-day family life?

The New You 13

It really is an exciting time for you right now! You will continue to grow physically and in your relationships with other people of both sexes, with your family, and with God. The days, months, and years just ahead of you are bright and exciting and full of opportunities to use what God has given you. God is with you every step of the way, strengthening, encouraging, and guiding you through His Word. The Holy Spirit gives you the power to live a new life each day full of confidence, knowing you are forgiven in Christ, free to serve others, and not burdened by fear or guilt.

The frustrations and disappointments will not end, but the joys and blessings will far outnumber them. You've reached the end of this book but not the end of learning about yourself and others. Take these few reminders with you as you go on from here:

1. Accept yourself as a worthwhile gift from God. You are special and unique.

2. You are worth the effort it takes someone to get to know you in a meaningful relationship. Don't settle for a relationship based on physical attraction only.

3. Thank God for the gift of your family. Pray for good communication. Know that they want what's best for you and are there to support you. Accept your family just the way they are. Forgive them and expect them to forgive you. Show them your love with words and with a hug now and then.

4. Thank God for your friendships. Pray for good Christian friends who will influence you positively. Reach out and help others. Be thoughtful toward them, and treat them the way you'd like to be treated.

5. Thank God for the special gift of marriage. Pray that God would

bless you with a partner to share your life with and that you would respect each other from the moment your relationship begins.

6. Thank God for your body. Work to keep it active and healthy. Take care of it, since it's the only one you'll have. Eat wisely, take time for rest and recreation, develop your special interests, and use the gifts God has given you.

7. Thank God for your special skills and talents. Work at those areas in which you can achieve. Strengthen the weak spots. Decide to be the best you can be at whatever you try, accepting your strengths and your limits.

8. Share your thoughts and ideas with others. Talk to them. Ask for advice, and don't be afraid to risk being fair, just, and Christian. Open up to those you admire and trust. Be honest with your parents and friends.

Critical Thinking:

- Why is important to stay connected to God through His Word, worship, and prayer during this time in your life?

- What type of daughter, girlfriend, wife, or mother do you hope to be?

Word List

Abortion (a-BOR-shun) Ending a pregnancy by killing the preborn child (embryo or fetus).

Abstinence (AB-stin-ens) To refrain from sexual intercourse.

Acne (ACK-nee) Pimples, blackheads, and other redness/inflammation on the skin. Acne is a common condition during adolescence. It can be caused by an overgrowth of skin and dead skin cells, clogged pores (hair follicles), oil production, and bacteria.

Adolescence (ad-uh-LES-sens) The period of life between childhood and adulthood; the teen years.

Adultery (ad-UHL-ter-ee) Sexual intercourse by a married person with someone other than his or her spouse.

AIDS (HIV/AIDS) A sexually transmitted disease that breaks down a person's immune system, damaging the person's ability to fight other diseases.

Androgynous (an-DROJ-e-nuhs) Genderless, having neither specifically masculine or feminine characteristics.

Anus (AY-nes) The opening where bowel movements leave the body.

Birth Control A method people who are having intercourse use to prevent pregnancy.

Cervix (SER-viks) The narrow outer end of the uterus.

Circumcision (ser-kum-SIH-zhun) An operation that removes the foreskin from the end of the penis.

Clitoris (KLIT-or-is) A small organ at the front of the vaginal opening that gives sexual pleasure when touched.

Conceive (kon-SEEV) To start a new life through union of a sperm cell with an egg cell; to become pregnant.

Condom (KON-dom) A thin rubberlike sheath placed over the erect penis before intercourse to prevent sperm from entering the vagina (to prevent pregnancy). Because of its high rate of failure, it does not provide a "safe sex" prevention of sexually transmitted diseases, as is often claimed.

Ejaculation (ee-jack-yoo-LAY-shun) The discharge of semen from the penis.

Embryo (EM-bree-oh) The unborn baby during the first eight weeks after conception.

Erection (ee-RECK-shun) The enlarging and hardening of a male's penis, usually during sexual excitement.

Fallopian Tube (fa-LOW-pee-an TUBE) The passageway connecting an ovary to the uterus. The fertilizing of the egg by the sperm normally takes place here.

Feminine (FEM-ih-nin) Something that is characteristic of women (the female gender). It refers to or describes something that women would have.

Fetus (FEE-tuss) The unborn baby after eight weeks or more in the mother's uterus.

Foreskin (FOR-skin) A fold of skin that covers the glans of the penis. (See Circumcision.)

Fornication (FOR-nih-KAY-shun) Sexual intercourse between unmarried people.

Gene (Jeen) A tiny part of a sperm cell or egg cell that carries characteristics from the father or the mother. Dominant genes are stronger than recessive ones and will have more influence over which characteristics are passed along to the baby.

Genital (JEN-i-tal) Pertaining to the sex organs.

Homosexuals (ho-mo-SEK-shoo-als) Men and women who experience same-sex attractions. They may or may not develop a gay identity and they may or may not act on their attractions.

Hooking Up Two people agree to get together for the purpose of making out or having sex; it does not imply there is or will be any relationship between them.

Hormones (HOR-mones) Powerful chemicals produced by the body to regulate growth and development. Circulate in the blood. Sex hormones affect the growth and function of the reproductive organs.

Hymen (HIGH-men) The thin membrane in a girl's body that covers the outside opening of the vagina.

Intercourse   (IN-ter-kors) (See Sexual Intercourse.)

Labor   (LAY-bur) The physical activities including contraction of the uterus and dilation of the cervix involved in giving birth.

Masculine   (MASK-u-lin) Something that is characteristic of men (the male gender). It refers to or describes something that men would have.

Masturbation   (mass-ter-BAY-shun) Sexual stimulation by handling or rubbing the genital organs.

Maxi Pad   (MAKS-ee pad) A soft pad used to catch the unneeded blood and waste tissue that flow from a woman's uterus during menstruation. Also called sanitary napkin or pad.

Menstruation   (MEN-stroo-AY-shun) The monthly flow of waste tissue and blood from the uterus. It is commonly called a period.

Miscarriage   (MISS-care-idg) The process through which a mother's body expels a baby that died in the womb.

Nocturnal Emission (nok-TER-nal ee-MISH-un) The release of semen during sleep, common in adolescent boys. Also called a "wet dream."

Orgasm   (OR-gazm) A series of pleasurable muscular contractions centered in the sexual organs and affecting the entire body.

Ovary   (OH-va-ree) The female reproductive organ in which egg cells develop and sex hormones are produced. Females have two ovaries.

Ovulation   (AH-vyu-LAY-shun) The discharge of a mature ovum from the ovary.

Ovum   (OH-vum) The egg cell created in the female ovary and released during ovulation.

Penis   (PEE-nis) The male sex organ that hangs between the legs and through which both urine and semen pass out of the body.

Period   (See Menstruation.)

Pituitary Gland (pih-TOO-it-air-ee gland) The body's master gland located at the base of the brain. Its secretions control and regulate many organs and influence most basic body functions.

Placenta   (pluh-SEN-ta) The organ that connects the fetus to the lining of the uterus by means of the umbilical cord.

Pornography (por-NOG-raf-ee) Books, images, or videos that show sex without a concern for God's Word or moral values. Shows or describes naked people or sex acts in degrading and sometimes violent ways in order to cause an emotional reaction.

Premature Baby (pree-mah-CHOOR BAY-bee) When a baby is born too early, before the usual nine months of growing in the uterus has passed.

Premature Ejaculation (pree-mah-CHOOR ee-jack-yoo-LAY-shun) A discharge of semen from the penis when a male sexual climax (orgasm) occurs before a man wants it to.

Prostate Gland (PRAH-state GLAND) A male gland that secretes fluid that mixes with sperm.

Puberty (PYOO-ber-tee) The time of becoming physically mature and being capable of reproducing, usually between ages 13 and 16 in boys and ages 11 and 14 in girls.

Safe Sex The false idea that intercourse with appropriate "safeguards" such as condoms will keep people from getting a sexually transmitted disease or from getting pregnant. The only safe sex is with an uninfected partner in a marriage where husband and wife are faithful to each other.

Scrotum (SKRO-tum) A bag of skin that hangs from the groin between the legs of a male. It supports and protects the testicles.

Semen (SEE-men) The male fertilizing fluid that is made up of sperm and the whitish liquid in which they flow.

Sexting (SEK-sting) The sending of sexually explicit messages or images on a phone or other device.

Sexual Abuse (SEK-shoo-uhl uh-BYOOS) Being touched inappropriately by an adult or peer.

Sexual Intercourse (SEK-shoo-uhl IN-ter-kors) The sexual union of a male and female; the inserting of the penis into the vagina.

Sexually Transmitted Disease (STD) Any of a variety of contagious diseases contracted almost entirely from sexual contact. The most common are HIV/AIDS, chlamydia, herpes, syphilis, human papilloma virus (HPV), gonorrhea, and trichomoniasis.

Sperm (SPERM) The male cell produced in the testicles to fertilize the female egg.

Sterility   (ster-ILL-it-ee) The inability to produce babies.

Tampon   (TAM-pahn) A small, pluglike piece of cloth (like cotton) that is placed into the vagina to catch the unneeded blood and waste tissue that flow from a woman's uterus during menstruation.

Testicles   (TESS-ti-klz) The two egg-shaped male reproductive glands where sperm are produced.

Transgender   (tranz-JEN-der) A person who perceives himself or herself to be other than his or her biological sex.

Transsexual   (tranz-SECK-shoo-uhl) A person who tries to look, dress, and act like a member of the opposite sex of how God biologically created him or her to be.

Transvestite   (tranz-VEST-iyt) A person who likes to cross-dress, wearing clothing that is typically worn by the opposite sex.

Umbilical Cord   (um-BIL-ih-kal KORD) The cord that connects the fetus to the placenta.

Urethra   (yoo-REE-thra) The tube through which urine passes from the bladder out of the body. In males, it also carries the semen.

Uterus   (YOO-ter-us) Also called the womb. The place where the fertilized egg develops into a fully formed baby.

Vagina   (vuh-JY-na) The passageway leading from the uterus to the vulva in a woman; the birth canal.

Virgin   (VER-jin) A person who has never had sexual intercourse.

Vulva   (VUL-va) The external female sex organ surrounding the genital opening.

Womb   (See Uterus.)

Zygote   (ZIE-goat) The fertilized cell immediately after conception.

Questions & Notes: